THE Next9en Librarian's survival guide

Rachel Singer Gordon

Information Today, Inc.

Medford, New Jersey

The NextGen Librarian's Survival Guide

Copyright © 2006 by Rachel Singer Gordon

Library of Congress Cataloging-in-Publication Data

Gordon, Rachel Singer.
  The nextgen librarian's survival guide / by Rachel Singer Gordon.
    p. cm.
  Includes bibliographical references and index.
  ISBN 1-57387-256-3
  1. Library science--Vocational guidance. 2. Library science--Vocational guidance--United States. 3. Librarians--Employment. 4. Librarians--Employment--United States. 5. Generation X--Emploment. 6. Generation Y--Employment. I. Title. II. Title: Next generation librarian's survival guide.
  Z682..35.V62G67 2006
  020.23--dc22

                                                                      2005036503

Printed and bound in the United States of America

President and CEO: Thomas H. Hogan, Sr.
Editor-in-Chief and Publisher: John B. Bryans
Managing Editor: Amy M. Reeve
VP Graphics and Production: M. Heide Dengler
Book Designer: Kara Mia Jalkowski
Cover Designer: Michele Quinn
Copyeditor: Pat Hadley-Miller
Proofreader: Caroline Kochanski
Indexer: Wendy Catalano

Contents

Acknowledgments

This book would not have been possible without the support of my editor, John Bryans; Managing Editor, Amy Reeve; and the rest of the dedicated staff at Information Today, Inc. As always, I appreciate their enthusiasm and their guidance. I am also indebted to the candor and insights of the many next generation librarians who took the time to contribute their perspectives through survey answers, interviews, and e-mails. I have done my best to represent their viewpoints and comments faithfully—any fault in interpretation is mine. Last, but definitely not least, I appreciate the patience of my two favorite guys—my husband Todd and my son Jacob—while I spent entirely too much time staring at the computer screen.

About the Web Page
www.lisjobs.com/nextgen/

This book references dozens of online resources for next generation librarians in all types of libraries (see Appendix B for a list of URLs by chapter). In recognition of the fact that Web pages tend to come and go, and in order to make *The NextGen Librarian's Survival Guide* more useful and enduring to its readers, these resources are listed and updated on one handy page.

Instead of typing numerous URLs into your Web browser, please visit www.lisjobs.com/nextgen/, where you'll find a clickable link to each site mentioned in the book.

Please feel free to e-mail any changes, comments, and suggestions to rachel@lisjobs.com.

Introduction

Recently, I found myself in a mentoring role with a relatively young former colleague who was seeking career advice ... Early in the conversation, he asked me what I thought he had to do to convince an older, more traditional business executive inside his company that he has the experience and know-how of someone much older. My answer: "Start building a time machine into the future. Your best bet is to age." "Well, what do I do right now?" he asked. "Keep getting older," I replied, half seriously.

Chad Dickerson[1]

We have spent a lot of time lately talking about issues facing next generation librarians ("NextGens"), whether in our literature, online, at conferences, or among colleagues. Topics range from a focus on the "graying of the profession" and the concurrent need for succession planning, to an ongoing push for recruitment and retention, to the comments and concerns of younger librarians and new grads about their experiences entering the profession. Given all the hype, one might think that now is the perfect time to enter the field—and, for many, it is. Those who find the right fit with a set of colleagues who share their professional excitement and concerns have entered the field at a fascinating juncture. They have the chance to impact their changing institutions and changing profession and to build the experiences they need to lead their libraries in the future.

Unfortunately, though, others find that the talk of upcoming shortages belies a currently tight entry-level job market, and that a number of libraries (and librarians) seem less than excited about what next generation librarians have to offer. The following pages discuss the challenges that next generation librarians face, some of which are unique to the under-40 age group, and some of which affect all librarians—new or experienced. NextGens will find discussion of various ways to survive, and thrive, in the 21st-century library environment, of ways they can capitalize on generational trends and assumptions, and of ways to recognize when generational issues are a factor and when they are irrelevant.

For the purposes of this book, next generation librarians will be defined as those currently in their 20s and 30s, part of the groups termed Generation X (born between approximately 1965 and 1978) and Generation Y (born approximately 1979–2000). (Observers define these ranges somewhat differently, and note a certain overlap at the edges; find more on defining generations in Chapter 1.) Those individuals older or younger than these somewhat artificially-imposed ranges can keep reading as well. Older recent grads may find much, if not all, of their experience reflected in these pages and long-time librarians can gain insight into the outlook and expectations of those newer to the field. Younger MLS (Master in Library and Information Science) students, potential librarians, and paraprofessionals will also be able to relate; the term "librarian" is not used exclusively to refer to individuals with an ALA-accredited graduate degree. In fact, chapters on topics like surviving library school will be particularly pertinent to NextGens who have not yet completed their MLS degree. Library administrators and managers can find insight into the concerns and outlook of their Generation X and Y employees, helping them overcome gaps in communication and understanding that can lead to workplace friction. A final chapter addresses administrators directly.

The problem of defining and labeling generations—especially those that self-consciously eschew labels—is well-documented and leads to such temptations as defining all Xers as slackers and Yers as self-centered. We need to look at general trends, rather than falling into simplistic stereotypes. What we can say, though, is that younger librarians share a certain commonality of experience that affects how they view the profession, how their colleagues view them, and their experiences in trying to break into the library field.

Our identity as people and as professionals consists of multiple and fluid factors: I am a member of Generation X; I am a mother; I am a librarian. These factors change over time. Three years ago, I did not have a child; 35 years from now I hope to be retired. This book takes an extended look at one of these factors: our status as GenX and GenY professionals and how it currently impacts both us and the field. It describes ways we can both learn from and move beyond generational differences, so that we can work together with our colleagues at all stages and levels to transform our profession and meet the needs of 21st-century library users. This book also recognizes that NextGens are the ones responsible for moving the profession forward over the next 20 to 30 years, giving them the responsibility to learn from and work with older colleagues now, while also discovering and planning where to go in the future. Tips are given for younger librarians entering this profession, who are dealing with colleagues who sometimes willfully deny that we are in an era of transition or that NextGens have much to contribute.

While the content inevitably reflects my own perspective and experiences as a Generation X librarian, I also have drawn upon the experiences and comments of a number of other next generation librarians through interviews, discussions, and e-mail groups such as nexgenlib-l and NEWLIB-L. Quotes and comments throughout the book come from two surveys that were posted online in January and February 2005—one for librarians, students, and library workers under age 40 and one for those age 40 and over. (Survey questions and a brief discussion can be found in Appendix A.) As Karen Schneider so simply points out in her observations on top technology trends in libraries, "information is a conversation."[2] The ideas in this book inevitably grew out of conversation with others.

The following pages look at questions like:

- What is unique about younger librarians' experiences?
- What do they share with older recent grads—and with all new librarians?
- What are NextGens' responsibilities to the profession?
- What can NextGen librarians do now to help move their institutions—and the field as a whole—forward?
- How can multiple generations work together effectively in today's library?
- How can NextGens avoid being their own worst enemies?

This is a "Survival Guide" for a number of reasons, ranging from many NextGens' growing disillusionment with certain aspects of librarianship as practiced in some institutions today, to the recognition that our profession is, in a number of ways, fighting for its own survival. Next generation librarians are those who are going to be around for the next few decades to deal with the aftermath of what we do now, and are those who will oversee the field's transformation in the future. As NextGen survey respondent Kam McHugh, Randolph Branch Manager, Memphis/Shelby County Public Library &

Information Center, Memphis, TN, puts it: " 'Next generation' involves thinking about the future of libraries and our profession beyond the next ten years or so. Many very good librarians in their 50s are thinking about the future of libraries too, but they realize that they most likely will be retired or nearing retirement. Younger librarians think about and plan for the future, knowing they will still be actively participating in the profession."

The chapters follow the natural progression of many younger librarians' careers, beginning with Chapter 1, on defining next generation librarianship. Chapter 2 focuses on surviving library school, and Chapters 3 and 4 provide tips on surviving the job hunt and entry-level positions. Progressing up the ladder, Chapter 5 covers moving forward into management or another institution. More general issues like image, stereotypes, and diversity are discussed in Chapter 6. Chapter 7 discusses making connections, and Chapter 8 talks about finding work/life balance. Chapter 9 takes a look at the ways in which next generation librarians might transform the profession, while Chapter 10 addresses current administrators interested in retention and succession planning. Appendix A contains the text of the two surveys used in the book, along with brief statistics and comments, while Appendix B provides a quick reference to the Web sites mentioned throughout.

I would love to hear your comments, ideas, and contributions to this ongoing conversation, and welcome any feedback at rachel@lisjobs.com.

Endnotes

1. Chad Dickerson, "What It Takes to Get Ahead," *Infoworld* Feb. 21, 2005: 22.
2. Karen Schneider, entry on the official PLA blog, January 16, 2005, www.plablog.org/2005/01/top-technology-trends.html, 19 January 2005.

1

Next Generation Librarianship

Each era has its own mood, a flavor or tone that pervades the developing perspective of youth. These messages—often invisible, especially at the time—have a profound effect on the generation as a whole. The individual members of a generation vary greatly ... But their shared experiences are what unite them as a generation. What binds them is the mainstream culture of the time that formed them—the media messages, news events, and national mood.

Claire Raines[1]

Why is next generation librarianship an issue now? Successive waves of younger librarians over the years have, of course, always moved into library workplaces, interacted with colleagues and patrons from different generations, and faced some of the issues that this book addresses. Several factors, though, put today's next generation librarians in a unique situation:

➤ The flattening of workplace hierarchies and the rise of participative management means that younger and greener librarians are participating on equal ground (or on the pretense or perception of equal ground) with their elder colleagues more often than they were likely to in the past.

➤ Technological change brings a need for new skills and a new way of looking at library services. Technological savvy is often people's first gut impression when thinking about NextGens' qualities, and while technological expertise and interest necessarily vary by the individual, this is an important perception for a reason. Growing up

1

with technology affects NextGens' perspective on and comfort with its use. While technical skills are by no means unique to younger librarians, the way they integrate technology into their lives, in general, often differs.

➤ Outside pressures on librarianship in the 21st century place younger librarians in a unique role. Beyond technology, we need to challenge existing perceptions of libraries and librarians, and show our continued relevance to various groups. NextGen librarians bring in new ideas and are often better able to relate to younger groups, drawing them in and involving them in their libraries.

➤ NextGens have more options open to them than many younger librarians and potential librarians had in the past. Much has been written about librarianship as traditionally a women's profession. Younger women who, in the past, might have become teachers, librarians, social workers, or nurses, now have more options. Librarianship must compete for a new generation of recruits on a different ground. As one under-40 survey respondent puts it, "[Younger librarians are] also not willing to accept what is given to them and realize that they only get what they ask for. They are more assertive. What is unique is that younger librarians have the opportunity to do this; Baby Boomers were only starting to break out of the restrictions placed on them due to their gender."

➤ Information skills are in demand and transferable; if traditional libraries are to keep younger workers, they need to find a way to remain attractive in the face of increased nontraditional opportunities.

➤ The graying of the profession makes it essential for library workplaces to retain and nurture their younger staff. Find more on this later in this chapter and in Chapter 10, but suffice it to say that those who want to ensure the future of a graying profession had best begin paying attention to its greenest entrants now.

➤ Changing generational expectations and experiences affect younger librarians' attitudes toward the profession and toward traditional practices in many library workplaces. These include changing expectations of work/life balance, a differing view on employer/employee loyalty, and a predisposition toward continuous challenges and lifelong learning.

➤ Budget cuts and the post-9/11 economy have been less than kind to libraries, resulting in a tight job market for new grads, less professional development funding, and other belt-tightening measures.

These and other changes require that we pay attention to generational issues, looking at intergenerational interactions in the library workplace and at trends affecting our professional future.

Next Generation Librarians

Before moving on to tackle the issues affecting next generation librarians, we need first to discuss what defines next generation librarianship. While some define it solely as an attitude, an outlook, a way of professional engagement, a function of recent library education, or a combination of other factors largely unrelated to age, the most common position (and the one taken here) is that age is an unavoidable factor. Our current age and prevailing generational stereotypes can be defining aspects in how our colleagues, supervisors, and patrons look at us. Shared generational experiences both affect our outlook and provide common ground; these formative experiences help create generational cohorts that share similar life experiences and attitudes. As currently younger librarians, NextGens will also be the ones in charge of our institutions in 20, 30, or 35 years; the foundation we build now affects how we will proceed and what our libraries will look like in the future.

While age never defines us completely, it is a factor (among others) worth examining. Throughout, the assumption is that we are talking about generational trends rather than subscribing to counterproductive generational stereotypes. We can each point to a 90-year-old technofiend or a 20-year-old Luddite, a buttoned-down 30-year-old or a tattooed and pierced grandmother, but this is beside the point. As Zemke, Raines, and Filipczak write: "We are all individuals; there are a multitude of ways each of us differs from all others in our generation or even from our own family group. To be effective with other human beings, we must know them as individuals—their unique background, personality, preferences, and style. However, knowing generational information is also tremendously valuable; it often explains the baffling and confusing differences behind our unspoken assumptions underneath our attitudes. The 73-year-old Web master who creates rock and blues digital music doesn't fit the stereotype of the World War II era senior citizen, yet he was forever touched—as were all members of his cohort—growing up during the Great Depression, hearing about the disaster at Pearl Harbor, and feeling the pride and patriotism that were part of the fabric of the mid-1940s."[2]

A focus here on issues of interest to next generation librarians, further, should not be interpreted as implying that none of these issues have importance for all librarians; nor is it intended to intensify the generational divide. We have an unfortunate tendency to assume that any discussion of generational issues aims to play one group against another, or is ageist in its intent. Addressing generational concerns, though, can lead to greater understanding of our inherent connections as library professionals, as well as of the differences in outlook or experience that lead to miscommunication. The discussion can help us understand where younger librarians' experiences are unique, and where they mirror and build on the experiences of Boomer and older colleagues. It can help older colleagues understand younger librarians' backgrounds and outlooks, enabling them to better manage, work with, and communicate with these younger colleagues. Throughout the book, the outlook of both younger and long-time librarians on various issues is reflected through comments and quotes.

We can think about our overlapping experiences and outlooks as real-life Venn diagrams, looking both at where they intersect and where they differ. This helps us avoid the trap of either thinking all of our experiences are unique to our age group or of overemphasizing age as the only issue. Looking at generational factors is one way to avoid interpreting everything through our own lenses.

Defining Generations

As Smith and Clurman explain: "Members of a generation are linked through *the shared life experiences of their formative years*—things like pop culture, economic conditions, world events, natural disasters, heroes, villains, politics, and technology—experiences that create bonds tying the members of a generation together into what social scientists were the first to call 'cohorts' (emphasis in original)."[3]

Different observers define generations somewhat differently; the beginning and ending dates vary somewhat and tend to overlap. The general agreement, though, is that today's workplace is comprised of four generations with these approximate birth years: Veterans (1922–1945), also called the Silent Generation, Great Generation, or World War II Generation; Boomers (1946–1964); GenX (1965–1978), also called Baby Bust; and GenY (1979–2000), also called Millennials, Net Gen, N-Gen, Nexters, or Echo Boomers. There is also general agreement on the age ranges, and on the fact that much of what comprises a "generation" is its members' shared experience of defining events and formative experiences—for example, the Veterans by World War II; the Boomers by Woodstock, the Cold War, and the moon landing; GenX by divorce, AIDS, and MTV; and GenY by the Internet and 9/11. Other factors include each generation's relative size compared to other generations, as well as simultaneous demographic shifts. Relative sizes of generations also translate into their relative representations in the workplace; the smaller Generation X is bookended by the larger Baby Boom and Generation Y groups.

Paying attention to generational trends helps us to communicate with different age groups and to see how our own experiences affect the way we perceive and react to situations. Realize that these can be both strengths and shortcomings; part of effective next generation librarianship means learning to realize where the tendencies created by shared generational experiences and outlooks can cause problems, as well as where they are assets. It also requires that we recognize that generational trends are just that, and respect expertise and enthusiasm wherever it can be found. Just as next generation librarians deserve to be judged on their own merits and by their own actions, so, too, do colleagues of all ages.

Younger librarians comprise those in both Generation X and Generation Y, and their approaches to the profession and the stereotypes they encounter from colleagues and patrons can differ. Some GenX librarians have more of a sense of being "in between" and of being part of the generation that connects older and younger librarians in their workplaces. One survey respondent in her 30s notes: "I sense that I'm fairly typical: someone who has worked in another field for around 10 years and is entering librarianship as a second profession. I feel as if I straddle both 'old' or traditional librarianship (I used card catalogs until college) and newer technologies and theories (I've worked on the Web for years and feel comfortable with and enjoy all the new ways of communicating). I like the idea of being a bridge between library theories and the world of technology we find ourselves in."

Many other GenX survey respondents also expressed that they felt themselves part of a group that is specifically able to bridge the gap between Baby Boomer and GenY librarians. One says: "Being nearly 40, I find myself bridging the gap between younger and older librarians." Nancy Renfro, Director, Watauga Regional Library Center, Johnson City, TN, echoes the same sentiment: "I feel somewhat like a 'bridge' librarian—somewhere between NextGen and traditional. I have enough of the old to know where traditional librarians are coming from, and enough of the new to understand where things are going, but I don't really feel part of either one." Valerie Nye, Public Library Consultant, New Mexico State Library, Santa Fe, shares: "Actually, I see GenXers as a bridge between the Boomers and the Millennials. Both the Boomers and the Millennials are huge generations. From what I understand, Generation X is fairly small. While I am interested in GenX issues, I really think the Millennials will have the bigger impact."

The gaps in experiences, expectations, and perceptions between a 38-year-old GenXer and a 24-year-old Millennial can be significant, as can the differences in the ways they are viewed by their co-workers, supervisors, and patrons. Some GenX survey respondents who are a few years into the profession were careful to differentiate their viewpoints from those they have heard their Millennial colleagues express. Michelle Swain, Director, Arkansas City Public Library, KS, says: "But you also can't discount life experience as an employee asset. Some very young MLS holders expect too much right out of the box."

Other survey respondents in their 30s see the difference even a few years of library experience makes in changing both their and others' perceptions, and talk of their excitement about now having the opportunity to mentor Millennials, who may be 10 to 15 years their junior. Adriana Edwards-Johnson, Serials, Electronic Collections, and Technical Processing Librarian, Southwestern Oklahoma State University, Weatherford, says: "Five years ago I was seen as a 'golden child' in my state. I was the youngest active and degreed librarian in the state association. I'm still younger than the majority of people in my state association, but there is a new group of 'youngens'—I have taken on a role as big sister to many of them." Janet Crum, Head, Library Systems and Cataloging, Oregon Health and Science University, Portland, says: "I think I'm on the cusp of the next generation. I've held professional positions for 12 years, have been a department head for three years, and often find myself mentoring library school students who do internships here. But I'm the youngest member of the management team, and still one of the youngest librarians here at OHSU. So I'm sort of in between, both professionally and socioculturally."

Others explain how their relationship to the profession differs from that of their Millennial counterparts. Some reject the term NextGen outright, believing it applies only to the youngest, brand-new librarians. Peter Bromberg, Program Development Coordinator, South Jersey Regional Library Cooperative, Gibbsboro, NJ, says: "I consider myself the bridge between NextGens and blue hairs. I'm young enough in age, lifestyle, outlook, etc., to share certain NextGen values and characteristics. But, with 11 years in the biz, I also have some experience under my belt, and have been able to form many relationships that probably set me apart from the NextGen experience of newbieness." When asked whether she considers herself a NextGen, Amanda Enyeart, Manager of Library Services, The Children's Hospital, Denver, CO, says: "I would have (if I had known the term) when I was in library school and looking for my first library job in the late '90s and early 2000s. I needed to feel somehow special and justify my choice of careers. Now I just consider myself a librarian."

In this, many GenX librarians express similar views to those of some Baby Boomer colleagues in their early 40s—showing how the lines between generations can become fuzzy, especially among those on the cusp. As Tina Hubert, General Consultant, Lewis & Clark Library System, Edwardsville, IL, says: "Well, I think I'm smack-dab in the middle. I'm too young to be really thinking and planning my retirement, and too old to be considered next generation. I am one of the people who bridges the generations and tries to help each other understand and respect the other generation's perspectives." Carolyn Davidson, Librarian/Library Consultant, North Texas Regional Library System, Fort Worth, TX, agrees: "Being right at 40, I feel I relate well to younger and older professionals. I think I tend to lean more with the younger professionals. I encourage change and innovation in a library; Internet cafes, databases, googling, and IM all have their relevance. The library profession is really morphing and we need to morph with it. I think some of the older librarians and professors just don't feel like being bothered. Libraries are seen as monuments to our democracy and society, which they are, but they need to be living monuments."

While "next generation" librarians comprise those in both GenX and GenY, sometimes their professional experiences and outlooks differ, as highlighted in these quotes; more of these instances will be pointed out in the pages that follow.

Retirement, Recruitment, and Reality

According to the U.S. Census 2000 EEO Data Tool, of the 184,745 people employed as librarians, 47,765 (26 percent) are aged 39 and under and 18,821 (10 percent) are aged 60 and over.[4] Factors that contribute to the unique age demographics of librarians include the relatively large number of Baby Boomers (and small numbers of GenXers) in the workplace in general; the fact that people tend to enter library school later in life, as a second career or after working in libraries for some years; and the shift in career options open to young women and the corresponding impact on a relatively low-paying female-dominated profession.

Data from various sources does support the view of librarianship as an aging profession, and there is agreement on an upcoming wave of retirements—though we are not quite clear on exactly when the peak of this wave will occur, or on its impact. A 1999 ALA survey, for example, shows only 26 percent of librarians are ages 20–39, consistent with 2000 Census results; 1990 Census and ARL data paint a similar picture of librarians being generally older than members of other comparable professional groups. ALA uses this data to suggest that we need to engage in increased and ongoing recruitment efforts to ensure the future of the profession; ALA's Web site notes that "… there is a need for sustained effort to recruit new people into the LIS professions and to retain those who are working in libraries today. As large numbers of LIS professionals reach retirement age, there is a corresponding need for new people to replace them."[5] The popular press repeats this assertion in countless stories about the upcoming librarian shortage and efforts to spur recruitment, including large IMLS (Institute of Museum and Library Services) grants toward recruitment efforts.

A brief January 2005 *American Libraries* article[6] notes that newer 2000 Census data do skew previously projected retirement trends forward somewhat. While originally expected to peak in 2010–2014 (based on 1990 data), the major wave of librarian retirements (based on an assumption of retirement at 65) is now expected from 2015 to 2019. The full report can be found online at www.ala.org/ala/ors/reports/recruitretire/recruitretire-adeeperlook.pdf; it makes no mention of the impact of a five-year shift in retirement predictions on current recruitment efforts. While Census data is an interesting and useful measure, ALA also notes that Census data is self-reported, and does not necessarily reflect actual numbers of MLS-degreed librarians. The newer ALA report describes a large influx of career changers, as has been typical in librarianship. As next generation librarians enter the profession, it is worthwhile to think about how the continued entry of mid-career grads with significant prior work experience affects both younger librarians' career prospects and the makeup of the profession.

It is also worthwhile to look at the current experiences of new grads who have recently been recruited to fill vacancies, which are anticipated to peak 10 to 15 years in the future. A number of grads report a very tight entry-level job market, and some of their concerns are shared throughout this book. Wilder points out that there has been a huge increase in MLS students over the past 20 years or so, resulting in an increase in job-seeking grads, and that their overall age is increasing: "While the overall number of MLS students nearly tripled between 1983 and 2001, the number of individuals under age 30 *decreased* 24 percent (emphasis in original)."[7]

Boomer librarians' retirement plans affect NextGen librarians both now and in the future. Boomer managers should think now about grooming NextGens for future leadership positions. Vast amounts of institutional memory will be lost in the predicted retirement wave and management and other upper-level positions will become more plentiful as librarians retire. ALA discussions refer to 65 as "traditional retirement age." Will turning 65, though, signify full retirement for the majority of Boomer librarians? A 2003 AARP study[8] found that 79 percent of Boomers now expect to continue working at least part-time after retirement, yet James Matarazzo's study of 1990 U.S. Census data shows the average age of retirement for librarians to be 63, and fewer librarians than in the past working after age 65.[9] Librarians in government or school positions are often eligible for early-retirement packages or buyouts long before 65—at 55 or 60—based on the number of years they have worked in a given system. Some organizations also offer early-retirement packages every so often to encourage long-term employees to leave and make room for younger, lower-salaried entry-level workers.

Other smaller or regional studies such as a 2003 Colorado survey on retention, retirement, and recruitment also show large numbers of current librarians planning to retire before age 65,[10] but do not seem to address the question of whether retiring Boomers will continue working part-time or volunteering in some library capacity post-retirement. As Anna Winkel, Branch Manager, Fraser Valley Library Branch of the Grand County Library District, Fraser, CO, notes of her own institution, "Most of my older colleagues work part-time as paraprofessionals. I think that they see this as a way to spend some time while enjoying semi-retirement." Kam McHugh, Randolph Branch Manager, Memphis/Shelby County Public Library & Information Center, Memphis, TN, says: "I think the 'crisis' of Boomer retirement that so many in our profession say is going to occur is overblown. Sure the numbers may say that many librarians are eligible for retirement, but how many will actually retire when the time comes? I know many librarians who enjoy their jobs so much they stay on well past their eligibility. I know of many who can't afford to retire or don't want to, so they can enjoy an even greater lifestyle when they do finally retire. I also know of people who retire from other fields who enter our profession in their early 50s planning to work another 15 years in the field."

As libraries continue to face budget crunches, part-time, experienced workers may be a very attractive pool to aid them in cost- and benefit-cutting. Also, financial uncertainties and Baby Boomers' wishes to remain productive during an anticipated lengthy retirement may see more librarians than in the past working in one way or another after retiring from their full-time positions. Some simply will not be able to afford to retire due to the bottom dropping out of their retirement plans and IRAs or due to spiraling health insurance costs; others will wish to continue to contribute to the field, even if in a reduced capacity. Further, the Colorado survey and others mention uncertainties as to what percentage of retiring librarians' positions will be retained; again, budget cuts and restructuring leave librarians with little guarantee that the number of slots for librarians will remain constant.

Writing about upcoming academic library retirements in *The Journal of Academic Librarianship,* Wilder outlines two possible paths. First, libraries will replace retirees at or near a one-to-one ratio, which will of course increase demand for LIS professionals as the expected retirement wave begins to hit. The second scenario, though, anticipates reduced numbers of librarians in the future. As he writes:

> A confluence of factors, however, makes another sce-nario at least as plausible. In this scenario, budgetary con-straints, automation, outsourcing, and the movement of tasks from librarians to support staff would reduce replacement demand to well below the one-to-one level. ... This scenario would quickly reduce the overall size of the profession, and leave demand for librarians stable at best. Those librarians who remain would experience a sharper distinction between their duties and those of support staff: Their jobs would be higher skilled, more managerial, and less routine, and reflect a wider pay gap.[11]

While no one can predict this with complete accuracy, there are a number of warning signs that point to a potentially troubled future. Find more on this in Chapters 9 and 10.

Data from other countries show a similar age pattern to that in the U.S. Australian data, for example, show 52 percent of Australian librarians over the age of 45; projections are that 40–60 percent will retire in the next 10–15 years.[12] This, of course, works from the same assumptions as the U.S. data: that people will retire at the expected age, and that the positions they vacate will be filled with full-time professionals.

NextGen or New Grad?

While most next generation librarians are by definition fairly new entrants to the profession, as mentioned in the previous section, ALA and other sources note that librarianship has been a traditional second or third career for many—and that this trend appears to be on the rise. New grads in their 40s and 50s who make a new career of librarianship do share a number of concerns and qualities with next generation librarians: Their education is more current; they are entering the same tight entry-level job market; and their experience with learning and using new library-related technology is more recent. Equating the two groups completely, though, is counterproductive, and fails to acknowledge generational differences.

Although new grads in general face a difficult entry-level job market, differing generational biases and experiences affect their early professional experiences. When hiring managers and search committees look at a new librarian in her 20s, their first thoughts may include "lack of experience," "won't be loyal to the organization," or "must be good with technology." When they look at a new librarian in her 50s, their thoughts may run along the lines of "will have trouble adapting to changing technology," "might have trouble shifting gears after 20 years in a different field," or "won't want to be groomed for management." This is not to say that these stereotypes are right, but we do need to understand that they exist, that they affect the reasons that people will or will not hire us, and that they affect the way we need to approach the job market and interviews.

Older new grads are more likely to enter librarianship as a second or third career, and their previous work and life experiences affect both their professional approach and their career prospects. Angelica Cortez, News Researcher, Fort Worth Star-Telegram, TX, explains: "My experience differs in that this is my first career. My older colleagues have already had careers, whether it be teacher, lawyer, parent, etc." These transferable skills can be an asset on the job market for older new grads, as another under-40 survey respondent mentions: "Where we differ, I think, is that [older grads] can more easily apply experience gained in other fields when arguing that they have what it takes to fill 'experience needed' positions than I can."

Some NextGens are energized by their second career colleagues, and point out the unique qualities they bring to the table. Suzanne Royce Cruse, MLS student, University of Denver, says: "[My] older colleagues are from other professions and have chosen library work because of a plethora of interests. I find them wonderful to work with because they have experience and ideas, so we don't re-invent the wheel." Part of what makes our profession so varied and exciting is the variety of experiences brought in by different groups, including career-changers, long-term paraprofessionals going back for their degree, and NextGens who come straight to MLS programs from their undergraduate careers and bring an alternative perspective. We can all learn through interaction with one another. Some next generation librarians do also come to the profession with years of experience, starting as a high school page and working their way up or holding down a paraprofessional position while earning a BA and graduate degree.

Some observers talk about next generation librarianship as being defined by an approach or an attitude, rather than as defined in any part by age. (Those experienced librarians or older new grads that feel this way can read on, and take from the following chapters what fits their situations.) Making a distinction between next generation librarians and new grads in general can also frustrate older new grads who feel they share commonly perceived NextGen qualities and skills, or irk long-term librarians who believe age is not, or should not be, a factor in our profession. Some librarians have expressed that the very term NextGen—and by extension this discussion—is ageist in its intent. A number of respondents to the over-40 survey shared similar views on this point, saying:

> ➤ "I suspect that the true next generation of librarians will be a blend of chronologically younger and older people, with incredible arrays of experience and interests, not least of which will be facility with, and interest in, technology and electronic resources. Learning to work well with others goes both ways, and starts with respect."

> ➤ "Interesting that using 'generational issues' changes this, for some, from age discrimination. Interesting that

because I am 64, I must have old ideas. Interesting that new and young is seen as so different."

➤ "I think that whether you are dealing with a post-modern view or not has a greater impact on librarianship than a person's chronological age. I am not trying to be a grump—but rather not be put into a box in which I don't belong."

➤ "Folks continue to conflate youth with being new to librarianship. A sizeable percentage of first time SLIS grads are not young, and stats prove this. Despite this, and despite the fact that I and others have complained and whined about this, we generally have our concerns ignored, minimized, or patronized. I don't think there is much difference among my peers of all ages who graduated around 2000. I cannot understand why you cannot distinguish between age at graduation and year of graduation, two unrelated concepts!"

➤ "I don't think you can infer anything about a group of professionals or generalize anything about a group of professionals' behavior based on age."

➤ "Age is often not the most relevant factor in determining values. At 60, I'm an avid computer gamer and have had wonderful conversations with teenage gamers once they discovered that I knew what I was talking about."

➤ "By your standards I am not NextGen, but I have all their qualities (except for grey hair and larger collection of Grateful Dead recordings). I've been using computers since before the NextGen librarians were born."

➤ "I'm not sure my age has anything to do with the profession. I know people of all ages who have a range of relationships with librarianship and I fit in that range. I really don't see a whole lot of difference by age."

Some under-40 respondents agreed with these points:

➤ "I do not consider myself a 'next generation librarian' because I work with librarians nearly twice my age who are just as forward thinking and in tune with the profession as myself. The defined lines of the generations do not reflect the knowledge or abilities of our profession. Instead, there are people from every generation who embrace or reject change."

➤ "I will say that 'next generation librarian', in my mind, doesn't refer to a specific age category, but rather a mindset. Individuals who are willing to embrace the basic theories of librarianship—but use new practicalities to implement the theory—thus inviting change."

➤ "Generational issues aren't always tied to age. I've worked with some very 'young' librarians who are on the brink of retirement and some 'old' librarians who have been working in libraries only a year or two longer than myself. Being a 'young' librarian is primarily a matter of attitude, not age."

➤ "I just consider myself a librarian. After being termed GenX for so long, I'm tired of being lumped together with others based on my age. Although a generation can have similar traits, it is unfair to make so many assumptions about someone based on their age."

➤ "I also feel that next generation librarian is a condescending label, that it has implications of a generation that expects to supersede its predecessors. The next generation of librarians is more than the 25–30-year-old graduates, it encompasses a whole set of people that vary in age and mindset. Fellow 2004 graduates over 45 are just as much 'next generation' as I am, simply because of the time and place of graduation in relationship to the profession."

These comments do show the need to think about our own assumptions and to understand that age is just one of a multitude of factors affecting our place in the profession. (Find more on generational stereotypes in Chapter 6, and more on intergenerational connections in Chapter 7.) These comments also point to the perception among many that any examination of generational differences inherently feeds ageism. When we talk about professional problems and concerns, we need to be careful of our language and mindful of these perceptions. We need, though, not to let these concerns stifle our discussion of generational issues. Thinking and writing and talking about NextGen issues should never fuel divisiveness; we all chose this profession, we are all in it together, and we all share the responsibility for moving it forward. The very point of looking at generational factors and assumptions is to improve our understanding of one another and our ability to work together in a 21st-century library, achieving our institutional goals and maintaining our professional strength. Talking about NextGen issues and outlooks does not imply that new librarians' issues and outlooks in general are of lesser importance.

As one under-40 survey respondent says: "There could be more emphasis on newer and older librarians working together and learning from each other in the general discourse. It's so useless to label, divide, say 'I love books and hate the way things are moving' or 'Books are dead, long live the Internet.' It's not either/or. If anything, I think it's exciting that we're finally opening up to providing different avenues into information for people, and we all need to work together to help facilitate this." Another has the last word on the subject, explaining: "While generational issues do need to be discussed and resolved, I am concerned about making too big an issue out of them. We do not want to draw a line between two generations of librarians and unintentionally alienate them from each other. Instead, we need to learn to work together as we seek to help librarianship evolve with the times to serve the needs of the public. Each librarian, new or experienced, old or young, brings valuable experiences, perspectives, skills, and ideas to the profession. We need to find a way to acknowledge those assets and put them to good use."

Endnotes

1. Claire Raines, *Connecting Generations: The Sourcebook for a New Workplace,* Menlo Park, CA: Crisp Publications, 2003: 11.
2. Ron Zemke, Claire Raines, and Bob Filipczak, *Generations at Work: Managing the Clash of Veterans, Boomers, Xers, and Nexters in Your Workplace*, New York: AMACOM, 2000: 14.
3. J. Walker Smith and Ann Clurman, *Rocking the Ages: The Yankelovich Report on Generational Marketing,* New York: HarperBusiness, 1997: 3.

4. Data can be accessed with the Census 2000 EEO Data Tool at www.census.gov/eeo2000/index.html.

5. Mary Jo Lynch, "Age of Librarians (1999)," American Library Association <www.ala.org/ala/hrdr/libraryempresources/agelibrarians.htm> 9 February 2005.

6. Mary Jo Lynch, "Recruitment and Retirement: A Deeper Look," *American Libraries* January 2005: 28.

7. Stanley J. Wilder, *Demographic Change in Academic Librarianship*, Washington, DC: ARL, 2003: 17.

8. Key findings, the full report, and a slide show are available online at http://research.aarp.org/econ/boomers_envision.html.

9. See James Matarazzo, "Library Human Resources: The Y2K Plus 10 Challenge," *The Journal of Academic Librarianship* 26:4 (July 2000): 223–224.

10. Nicolle Steffen, et al., *Retirement, Retention, and Recruitment: The Future of Librarianship in Colorado,* Denver: Library Research Service, September 2004 <www.lrs.org/documents/closer_look/RRR_web.pdf> 12 February 2005: 3.

11. Stanley J. Wilder, "Generational Change and the Niche for Librarians," *The Journal of Academic Librarianship* 22:5 (Sept. 1996): 386.

12. Sue Hutley and Terena Solomons, "Generational Change in Australian Librarianship: Viewpoints From Generation X," paper presented at ALIA 2004, 21–24 Sept. 2004 <http://conferences.alia.org.au/alia2004/pdfs/hutley.s.paper.pdf> 29 January 2005.

2

Surviving Library School

And the fact that we do hate school is a very good thing. It means we're still alive.

Derrick Jensen[1]

The first step for many younger librarians and aspiring librarians lies in choosing, getting into, and surviving their tenure in library school. This holds true whether you believe in the intrinsic value of a library education in broadening your perspective and professional outlook, giving you the skills you need to succeed, and providing the theoretical foundation for your work, or whether you have found that you just need to get that "union card" to progress in your career. (This is an ongoing professional argument; find more discussion of the need for the MLS in Chapter 9.) It is a given that many libraries will hire you faster, promote you more willingly, and treat you as a professional only if you have your ALA-accredited MLS. If you have already earned the degree, it may be interesting to see if the following discussion matches your experience, or you can skim or skip to Chapter 3.

Library school can be an interesting experience in and of itself. In my very first class, on my very first day, my very first professor (who has since retired) got a short way into his introductory lecture, paused, and said something along the lines of: "Well, they don't really do it this way in libraries any more, but this is the way we've always taught it here, and the way this course is structured." I spent the rest of that period doing the math on what that course would cost me per hour. An unfortunate number of next generation librarians share similarly disappointing introductions to the profession. Academia can be sluggish in responding to the ongoing practical changes in any field, and some long-tenured professors seem to have almost alien outlooks and experiences to those of their much younger students. One under-40 survey respondent expresses a rather bleak viewpoint on library education and the way it prepares (or fails to prepare) graduates for the real-world job market: "I am of the opinion that under-funding of LIS schools, a shortage of full-time library school faculty, and lack of a standard LIS curriculum is to blame for the widely varying skill levels of candidates currently looking for jobs in the library marketplace."

Many library schools are currently in transition and have been experiencing competing pressures for the past 10 to 15 years. There is no real agreement on what a library education should look like; different commentators suggest differing improvements, and different schools have varying foci and strengths. The wide variety of potential careers for information professionals, ranging from school media specialist, to foreign monographs cataloger, to competitive intelligence specialist, to knowledge manager, also creates a burden for schools in defining a core curriculum and satisfying the competing needs of their students and their future employers. Many also suffer from a tension between teaching or focusing on "information" or "library" science; some have dropped the "L" word altogether amid a storm of controversy.

Over-40 survey respondent Allison G. Kaplan, Assistant Director of the Education Resource Center and Coordinator of the School Library Media Specialist Program, School of Education, University of Delaware, Newark, summarizes many people's concerns about these tensions: "I am concerned about the perceived differences between librarianship and information science. I do believe this is a generational issue as well as a problem with stereotypes. I also believe that much of this problem begins in the library schools themselves when students are forced to make a choice between the two branches. I have a hard time seeing the difference because, at a very basic level, it's all about information. I believe that technology, computer science, and information systems, have had, in a sense, a detrimental effect on the profession by creating an artificial divide. Whatever issues we pursue in librarianship, our goals are the same: to improve information access and the literacy levels of our patrons. If I pursue that goal by reading to children, it doesn't make me less important in the profession than the person who pursues the goal by creating new information retrieval systems. This is a pressing issue and needs to be addressed."

Students, or potential students, take heart: Over the last few years, a number of schools have begun to respond to both internal and external pressures, modifying their curricula and their approach to attract new students and reflect recent changes in the profession. Those students lucky enough to have caring professors who have kept up-to-date with professional issues and trends will be better-prepared for their library careers, and will likely graduate with a more positive professional outlook. If you are considering library school, though, because you think it will lead to an easier career, shorter hours, assured employment, or a job where you get to read all day, think again! Sign up for some library-related e-mail lists, do some informational interviews, keep an eye on the job ads, and talk to current MLS students and working librarians to get a realistic picture of the profession and your prospects before applying.

If you are moving directly from college to an MLS program, understand that many, if not most of your fellow students will be older career changers or long-time library paraprofessionals going back to earn their degree. This generational mix in classrooms can be interesting and fruitful; you may find that at times you learn more from the experiences your fellow students bring in than from your assigned coursework. At the very least, you should appreciate the opportunity to benefit from their perspectives and input. ALISE (American Library and Information Science Education) Statistical Reports from the last few years include data on students' ages at various schools, as well as a number of other interesting library education-related statistics; access these online at http://ils.unc.edu/ALISE/.

The following sections discuss ways of minimizing the tensions in your own academic career, providing ideas for surviving—and even thriving in—library school. Attention to your professional development during your library school tenure, both in class and out, can set the tone for your professional career. Take this seriously, and jump full-steam into our fascinating profession!

Library School as a NextGen Issue

There are a number of factors that make surviving library school an issue of particular importance to NextGen librarians:

> ➤ NextGen librarians, especially Millennials moving directly from an undergraduate program to library school, may have more difficulty seeing their older professors as future peers and professional colleagues. Some are also more timid about building the relationships with their professors that can help jumpstart their library careers.

> ➤ NextGens lacking library—or even general—work experience can be at a disadvantage, compared to fellow

students who can bring their previous experience into the classroom.

➤ Some under-40 survey respondents feel that their professors were better able to connect to older students, which positively impacted the quality and tone of their educational experience. Carolyn Blatchley, Training Services Coordinator, Cumberland County Library System, Carlisle, PA, notes: "Older colleagues just entering the profession have had the same classroom learning experience, but often different experiences from a social aspect. The second-career students had closer relationships with professors (who tend to be of that same generation), and had opportunities to network and make many local connections."

➤ Younger librarians today are entering both an educational system in transition and a profession in transition, which affects their outlook and experiences and differentiates their library school tenure from that of colleagues who attended some time ago.

➤ Next generation librarians' general facilities with online communication allow them a unique avenue with which to research even remote institutions before applying. Further, the explosion of distance education opportunities in recent years creates a new way to earn the degree and opens up new possibilities.

➤ Younger librarians face the age-old gap between theory and practice during their academic careers. This is, of course, a long-standing tension in any library school, but can be exacerbated by the contrast in outlook between down-to-earth, impatient GenX and Y students and their older ivory tower professors.

➤ Younger librarians who have recently graduated college are likely to still be paying back student loans and additional loans taken out for grad school can add to this burden and make salary a paramount concern post-graduation.

Some of the following discussions will be applicable to all MLS students, while some are NextGen-specific.

Researching Schools and Classes

While applying to schools, examine the currency of their programs and of faculty members' research. Take a look at when, where, and on what topics their faculty are publishing. Look at the adjunct and full-time faculty mix. Your preferences here may vary: Some prefer the real-world experience adjuncts tend to bring, while others look at the percentage of full-time faculty as indicative of a school's commitment to the program. Look at the mix of courses the school offers, and examine professors' syllabi, which are usually now on the Web. Take a look at requirements and current course schedules as well as the official catalog, to see if classes of interest are actually offered at reasonable intervals and doable times. Since each library school has a different—if sometimes unofficial—focus, status, student mix, professor mix, and set of strengths, you will need to hone your information-seeking skills, and do your research as a precursor to even beginning the degree.

Here, you can use both official and "unofficial" channels. Official sources of data include the previously mentioned yearly ALISE Statistical Reports (http://ils.unc.edu/ALISE/) and ALA's list of accredited programs, which also links to the sites of individual schools (www.ala.org/ala/education/accredprograms/accreditedprograms.htm). Understand that there is, however, little standardization between schools, the rigor of their programs, and their foci; ALA accreditation just sets basic standards (www.ala.org/process/). You can also check with specialized associations to ascertain schools' foci and suitability for your needs; the Medical Library Association (MLA), for example, keeps its own list of schools offering health sciences librarianship coursework (www.mlanet.org/education/libschools/index.html).

Potential library school students are better prepared than other graduate students to research their schools of choice; the sharing spirit among librarians gives you a built-in network to pump for information on schools, classes, professors, and specialties. Start your librarian career early by taking the time to do your research and locate the school that will be best for you; every student enters with a different set of priorities. If your intent is just to get that piece of paper, then you might think about a commuter campus where you can get your degree within a year with minimum fuss, or look for the cheapest in-state program available. If you are not geographically mobile, and lack a school—or school you prefer—in reasonable commuting distance, talk to people currently enrolled in distance education (DE) programs. These vary widely in quality, content, technical requirements, technical support, cohort- and community-building support, and requirements for on-campus stays. Some rely heavily on asynchronous communication avenues such as online forums and e-mail; others use synchronous formats such as chat and interactive video that will require your online presence or presence at a local videoconference center at specific times. If you have specific interests, find a program and/or professor that specializes in a particular area. Do not just trust a school's published catalog; classes it lists may be rarely offered and might not even appear during your tenure.

As you might expect, online discussion groups, e-mail lists, and other collaborative Internet resources often host extensive and enlightening conversations about the qualities of different schools. Places that allow aliases tend to garner some frank discussion. Online forums are particularly useful if you are considering a distance education or distant program, where you may not have a local network of personal contacts to pump for information. You will also need to look at unique online DE factors such as university library access and tech support issues, as well as at your own aptitude for this type of learning and willingness to put extra effort into building connections with students and professors. Aspiring and new students may want to subscribe to librarian_wannabes (http://groups.yahoo.com/group/librarian_wannabes/), an e-mail group for potential and current MLS students in which members share their experiences with and questions about different schools, DE programs, specializations, and so on.

If, for whatever reason, you are limited to attending or interested in a particular school, you can also look for particular contacts at that institution. Again, online resources can help. Students in several programs have set up their own independent forums; see San Jose State University's SLIS Student Union (www.miraflor.tv/bbs/) for one example. Discussions range from the attributes of particular professors to suggestions of what classes to take in what order. Another tactic is to ask on newer librarians' discussion lists (such as nexgenlib-l or NEWLIB-L; find more in Chapter 7) for off-list input from students and recent grads, or search lists' archives for previous discussions.

Finding Community at LiveJournal

LiveJournal hosts a number of thriving library-related communities that regularly contain questions about and discussions of particular schools. These include:

➤ IU (Indiana University) SLIS, www.livejournal.com/community/iu_slis/

➤ Librarians in Training, www.livejournal.com/community/libraryschool/

➤ Library Grrrls, www.livejournal.com/community/library_grrls/

➤ Library Lovers, www.livejournal.com/community/libraries/

➤ Librarygrads, www.livejournal.com/community/librarygrads/

(Some LiveJournal communities also have associated RSS feeds, for those who prefer to follow through their aggregators.) These communities are a great way to get in touch with recent grads of or current students in particular programs, and to get honest feedback on schools' strengths and weaknesses. Topics range from recommendations of good online programs, to specific schools' support for internships, to professors and programs to avoid; the comment feature allows multiple participants to chime in. Once you graduate, think about giving back to the community by providing your own honest opinions and experiences to future students.

Go into your electronic research with the understanding that those who take the time to post most actively about their experiences may be those most frustrated with their graduate school tenure. Some discussions are skewed heavily toward the negative, so balance what you read online with your own research and impressions. These communities do, though, open up avenues for you to connect with students and recent grads, and to benefit from others' perspectives and experiences. We all know that a school's official line (or *US News & World Report* ranking) often bears little relation to the realities of its students' experience; NextGens have opportunities to share their experiences, a benefit not available to many of their older colleagues.

Look also at student professional involvement. Is there an active student organization? A student ALA chapter? Is this important to you, or are you already professionally active and/or employed and just looking for a commuter school where you can earn your degree with minimum fuss? If your student chapter is moribund, you and your fellow students may be able to revitalize it with the help of ALA/NMRT's Student and Student Chapter Outreach (SASCO) committee. Realize that it may be more difficult to participate in student organizations when enrolled in a DE program, although the convenience and/or the opportunity to attend a highly regarded nonlocal institution might outweigh these considerations. Further, the need to stretch yourself to actively network and participate as a DE student can be of use later if you are in a remote or underfunded library that offers few in-person networking opportunities. Active student organizations, though, offer you the opportunity for professional participation and to earn points for your resume while still in school. Take any opportunity to interact with your fellow students. The LIS field is a small one, and these people will be co-workers, colleagues, references, or bosses later on.

Identify the level of career support a school provides for both students and alumni. Does the library school have a separate career center, or is it subsumed in the career center for the entire university? What services does this office offer—a job bank, internship opportunities, career fairs? Do you get a sense of how area employers view the school's graduates? In a distance ed program, try to see whether career services are targeted locally or if they can help in your geographic area as well. Look at on-campus professional development opportunities: Do the program or student groups sponsor speakers? Hold workshops? Offer programs and continuing education opportunities for alumni?

Your initial contacts with schools can also be enlightening. Does the registrar's office get back to you promptly? Is the financial aid office communicative? How much red tape is involved in the application process? First impressions are important for a reason, and if a school seems uncommunicative or rude or bureaucratic before they even have your money, this can be a red flag.

Paying for It All

One sad truth of our less than high-paying profession is that those who take out extensive and expensive loans for library school can find themselves still paying these back years later, while also trying to live on salaries that often seem to assume a second household income. Younger librarians who have recently finished their BAs are also still likely to be paying off undergraduate loans; and, while going back to school can defer existing loans, adding more debt on top of what you already owe can be a daunting prospect. As with any higher education expense, try to minimize loans and maximize other aid. (See the sidebar on page 26 for some scholarship resources.)

When researching schools, cost can be a major factor. It may help to realize that most U.S. library employers look only for the ALA-accredited degree, not at the reputation of any specific school. The relative prestige of your school matters little when looking for employment, although the strength of a particular focus may matter in giving you the skills you need to succeed once you are on the job.

At state schools, the difference between in-state and out-of-state tuition can be significant. If you have a specific school in mind, you may want to relocate at least a year in advance of applying in order to establish in-state residency; be prepared to document your residence and show reasons other than school for moving, as schools can get picky on this point. Also look at schools that participate in programs like the Academic Common Market, which offers in-state tuition at selected participating institutions and programs to residents across multiple states.

Those for whom librarianship is a long-term goal and who can afford to be patient can think about taking the paraprofessional approach. A number of libraries will reimburse tuition for employees earning their MLS, LTA (Library Technology Assistant degree), or professional certifications, and working in a library while earning your degree also gives you resume fodder and much-needed experience. There are, of course, some strings attached; you may be required to have worked at an institution for a year or more before applying for tuition reimbursement, to keep a certain GPA, and/or to remain at your current institution for a set period of time post-graduation. If these requirements make you feel trapped, consider another approach. The specific stipulations

Scholarship Resources

Never start an MLS program without checking for local scholarship opportunities; state libraries, state associations, and local library systems often offer substantial aid for those planning to stay and work at an in-state library for a certain period of time post-graduation. Examples include Illinois' $7,500 "Training Grant for The Master of Library and Information Science Degree," which is contingent on LSTA (Library Services and Technology Act) funding and requires two years of local service within three years of graduation. Your state may offer a similar program.

Some selected national scholarship opportunities from major associations are identified in the list that follows. Check also with specialized associations in your area of interest to see if there are scholarships for particular subfields. Also consult ALA's "Financial Assistance for Library and Information Studies" (www.ala.org/ala/hrdr/educprofdev/financialassistance.htm) annual directory, which compiles awards from state agencies, local libraries, associations, academic institutions, and foundations:

➤ American Association of Law Libraries (AALL) Scholarships, www.aallnet.org/services/scholarships. asp
   Several different scholarships to fund MLS or law school studies.

➤ American Library Association (ALA) Scholarships, www.ala.org/Template.cfm?Section=scholarships
   ALA links to all its available scholarships and provides a common application and online references form.

➤ Beta Phi Mu Scholarships and Fellowships, www.beta-phi-mu.org/scholarships.html
   Several scholarships for MLS programs, continuing education, foreign study, or dissertation assistance.

➤ Medical Library Association (MLA) Grants and
Scholarships, www.mlanet.org/awards/
grants/index.html
    A number of different scholarships for MLS
programs, research, and continuing education.

➤ North American Serials Interest Group (NASIG)
Awards, www.nasig.org/awards
    Includes a scholarship for incoming MLS students
interested in serials librarianship.

➤ Special Libraries Association (SLA) Scholarship
Program, www.sla.org/content/learn/scholarship/
index.cfm
    Provides awards for graduate study leading to a
master's, graduate study leading to a PhD, and for
post-MLS study.

    Individual schools also often offer scholarships to
incoming students (check their Web sites or with their
financial aid offices), as well as financial aid or work-
study options. You may not be able to see the full range
until you apply or are accepted, but always ask.

should be spelled out in your policy-and-procedures handbook; some libraries will also list "tuition reimbursement" as a benefit in their job ads. Academic institutions often offer tuition reimbursement to all employees; consider working for a time in any position at a campus with a library school.

Some institutions do have a shortage of librarian-level positions, are cutting back on more highly paid professional staff, or suffer from the "once a paraprofessional, always a paraprofessional" mindset. So, keep in mind that earning your degree is not always a guarantee of the opportunity to move up in a given institution. As *Library Journal* (*LJ*) notes, though, a significant number of new grads do continue with their pre-MLS employers post-graduation, often moving up the ranks by combining their experience with their new degrees. *LJ's* October 2004 "Placements and Salaries" article, working from 2003 data, notes: "Of the 1140 graduates who reported full-time placement, 34 percent indicated that they returned to their employer as professional staff after graduation. Many of these graduates indicated they received salary increases and position upgrades upon completion of their master's degree, moving from a paraprofessional or technician position to a professional one."[2]

An earlier *LJ* article states that most MLS students originally come from the paraprofessional ranks, convinced by their experiences working in libraries to go back and earn the degree. "Libraries are the sources of most recruits to the profession and to the graduate programs that offer the necessary master's degree, the credential that transforms a library worker into a librarian. Most students study part time and work full time in libraries."[3] Some libraries do guarantee paraprofessionals advancement and/or raises once they earn their degrees, and a number make a point of filling most of their entry-level positions by "growing their own"—which becomes another factor affecting the job market for those taking a different approach. This is more common in public libraries; some academic libraries find themselves inundated with graduates from their own school and specifically seek candidates with degrees from other institutions to diversify their pool. (See Chapter 3 for more on job hunting.)

Any work experience during school, paraprofessional or otherwise, will enrich your classroom experience (and vice versa), allowing you to bring your real-world experience to class and to test out classroom theories and concepts at work. (See more on combining work and school later in this chapter.)

Making the Most of Your Time

During our academic careers, most of us itch to get out and have the chance to utilize what we have learned in "the real world." Once we are out, though, we often realize just what we missed out on during our time in school. If you are in school now, or are contemplating attending, think about ways to maximize your time while attending.

Chrissie Anderson Peters

Can you talk a little bit about your grad school experience—how you decided on a school, and how you made the most of your time there?

Initially, I applied to a couple of really high-ranked schools (one private and one where I would have had to pay out-of-state tuition), and was accepted at both, but then realized that the amount of time that I would have to work to make those programs worth the monetary investment was staggering. At the time, I lived in Virginia, so I could have chosen several different programs through the Academic Common Market and still gotten in-state tuition. The University of Tennessee (UTK), though, was beginning a totally online approach to their MSIS degree and I'd just been offered a job at Bristol Public Library (a system that crosses the Virginia state line and includes Bristol, TN). It just seemed to be meant for me to do the program at UTK—and I couldn't be happier about the education and opportunities that I received through that program. It may not have been ranked very highly by *US News & World Report*, but it is ALA-accredited; in the long run, that's the one true thing in terms of future employment!

What tips do you have on balancing grad school with full-time employment?

Be prepared to operate on only a little sleep! No, seriously, it was very manageable—most semesters. There were two semesters when I even took three graduate courses while working full-time. You have to be willing to apply yourself—manage your time wisely, which includes no goofing around online or sitting in front of the TV when you ought to be working on a paper or lab report, as well as using your breaks and lunchtime to read assignments and work on projects when necessary.

Additionally, learn to be creative. If you have a choice of project or paper topics, try to work them into something that your employer will allow you to do as part of your daily job. For example, in Collection Development, I created a regional collection of ghost stories and was permitted to work on it on the job because it might be something that the library would create itself at some point. UTK also offered occasional classes on weekends or for one week during the summer that were in line with my interests. These included storytelling for five Saturdays throughout the semester (and papers and online communications, as well as on-my-own practicing outside of those five on-site sessions); YA (Young Adult) literature during four weekends with other work required; a weeklong course offered one summer by children's author Jack Gantos (several folks shared the expenses of food and hotel rooms to take advantage of this opportunity, from all across Tennessee and Virginia, not all within driving distance of Knoxville, that involved tons of reading preparation beforehand and writing follow-ups afterward); and a Genre Fiction/Readers Advisory course that met on-campus for four weekends with outside projects and work required.

Probably most importantly, know if you've bitten off more than you can chew—although UTK wanted us to take two classes each fall and spring, many people realized after the first semester that this simply would not work, and decreased the workload to one class per semester. It took them longer to finish, but they still got to enjoy their families and fulfill commitments while continuing to work on their degrees.

How do you feel your distance education classes prepared you professionally?

I don't think that my education was compromised at all by having DE courses vs. on-campus experiences. It was incredibly useful to learn something in class, then go to work the next day and put it into practice. Also, we were able to discuss our day-to-day experiences in terms of various parts of the general theory of the profession. I had so many tools and resources at my disposal as a student that we did not have in our library that I was occasionally offered special projects on the job. These allowed me to help out with something there, while also honing my searching skills in a particular database—or even tying the two together to work on class assignments on the job. Additionally, I think that I'm pretty well-adjusted to online cooperation and group projects now and take advantage of those skills through involvement with state and national professional association committees where we might not meet face-to-face, but hammer out details of events or procedures via e-mail and online group meetings. We are in the information profession, and being able to use technology to share, exchange, and acquire information is part of what most of us do daily—my online DE classes just helped me be better prepared for it!

In what ways did you become professionally involved while in library school? What advantages did that bring?

As a DE student, I was part of what was termed "the Pioneers" cohort, the first class to have the option to do the program totally online. There were not many opportunities to be involved with campus/student chapters of our state or national professional associations.

However, being a student member of state associations like VLA (Virginia) and TLA (Tennessee) did afford me opportunities to co-present at conferences, talk with folks interested in pursuing their degrees (whether at UT or elsewhere), and get involved as time/opportunities permitted. During my time in graduate school, I became very involved with ALA, particularly with New Members Round Table (NMRT) and Young Adult Library Services Association (YALSA). I was chosen by then-Dean of UTK SIS, Dr. Elizabeth Aversa, to represent the SIS program at ALA 2001 in San Francisco (from a pool of applicants—not because of my GPA or anything strictly academic).

From that moment on, I took advantage of every opportunity I could in ALA! NMRT was particularly easy to be an active part of as a student, as there are several committee opportunities available for those who might not get to go to conferences and because anyone who wants to be on an NMRT committee can be! I ended up chairing the first committee I volunteered for in NMRT half-way through the year, and was elected as Secretary of NMRT while still a student. Getting involved with YALSA happened as a direct result of being recommended by Ed Sullivan, who had taught our YA Lit program—and who happened to be on YALSA's Board at the time.

I networked and made connections with professionals who offered opportunities to write about my experiences and share them with others in the profession. I took classes taught by Dr. Carol Tenopir, one of the most celebrated IS professionals of our time! My advisor from SIS, Dr. Jinx Watson, is on Dolly Parton's Dollywood Foundation's board of educators, responsible for selecting books for the Imagination Library program nationwide. (I still communicate with both Dr. Tenopir and Dr. Jinx, even though I graduated from SIS more than two years ago.)

All of those opportunities have taken me to "places" that I could never have imagined before graduate school. (Geographically, for conferences, but also in terms of professional development experiences like committee work, being published online and as part of Priscilla Shontz's *Librarian's Career Guidebook* crew, and even recently receiving my first payment for professional writing for a reprinted article.) I have met some of the greatest people in the world, not only in the field/profession, but through the opportunities presented to me in graduate school. I still keep in touch with my fellow Pioneers, and we have even started a scholarship at UTK's SIS—"the Pioneer Award"—to offer financial aid to others seeking their degrees through DE, as our class had no such financial aid opportunities. Life—professionally or personally—doesn't get much better than this!

Chrissie Anderson Peters, 33, is Librarian at Basler Library, Northeast State Community College in Blountville, TN.

In great part, we have the ability to make of our schools what we need them to be, just as we often later can take steps to get what we need out of our first jobs. Your outlook, goals, and activities throughout your graduate career play a large role in defining your later professional career. Emulate the approach of some of your older career-changing peers; as one explains: "In being in library school now, I am one of the oldest students in the class. This makes me not 'afraid' of the professors, and I can approach them as equals, rather than demigods to hold in awe. This helps my learning process, as I'm not as hesitant to ask questions or participate in the learning process as I would have been 20 years earlier." This can be difficult for NextGens, especially those right out of an undergraduate program. Realize, though, the more proactive you are in building relationships with your professors, actively participating in class, and asking challenging questions, the better your educational experience and the better your chances of finding mentors and beginning to build a professional network.

Also consider taking a variety of courses. Even those that seem of less interest now can be useful later—we have no guarantee of where we will end up, or the direction our careers might take. Experimenting with different coursework can help you see where your true interests lie, especially if you have not yet determined your desired subfield of librarianship. As you get closer to graduation, you can work on focusing your coursework and your professional activities. Post-graduation, though, you may at first end up "where the jobs are," rather than in your preferred niche. If you have your heart set on a particular type of librarianship from the outset, you might want to focus more heavily on relevant courses—but realize that these things do not always work out as planned. If you currently work in a library and just want to move up in your current institution or field, your existing experience will also help you focus. If you have a BA in an in-demand field (the sciences, IT), your previous education or experience may help you narrow down your focus earlier. If you have specific goals such as school librarianship, the need to earn a teaching certificate simultaneously with the MLS creates a straight and narrow path.

Aside from coursework itself, the more professionally active you can be during your graduate career, the better prepared you will be to enter the field—and the more likely you will be to grab a desirable entry-level position. (See Chapter 3 for more on job hunting.) As Matt Wilcox puts it: "You are a recent MLS graduate and I look at your resume/cover letter and I see what? That you went to library school. Okay, good, you have the absolute minimum requirement. Anything else? Did you work at a library while in school? An interesting internship or practicum? Anything at all that stands out?... Even if I am an enlightened search committee member, and we are trying to hire a fresh newbie because we want new ideas and to help someone get established, I still want to hire someone who did more than just show up."[4] Many hiring managers and search committees share a common perception that graduate school provides just the minimum requirements, and show a definite preference for those who take the initiative to gain other experience.

While some see comments like Wilcox's as condescending, or believe that a graduate school's responsibility is, in essence, to prepare students for entry-level positions, it really comes down to this: If this is what search committees and hiring managers want, it is what you need to do. Everyone graduates with that "piece of paper"; anything extra you bring to the table is an asset. When libraries have the luxury of picking among multiple qualified candidates for entry-level positions, you need to be proactive from the beginning. Tom Bahlinger points out: "Come job hunting and graduation time, what will separate your resume from those of your classmates: A 3.5 GPA ... a 3.7 ... a 4.0? No! Just about every graduate will have a high GPA. Experience will make your resume stand out, so my advice to library students is: *Get some library work experience!* (emphasis in original)"[5]

Barbara Lovato-Gassman explains why these extra steps are necessary from a library employer's perspective: "Employers would like to hire librarians with practical skills as well as theoretical knowledge. Since most library schools today do not focus on providing graduates with these practical skills, it is up to librarians to gain these skills through whatever means necessary: part-time employment, internships, additional course work (if available), and so on, before seeking a professional position."[6] This makes even more sense in comparison with other professions that make experience a priority—public schools will generally not hire a teacher who has not yet completed her student teaching; law students know that summer internships are their tickets to later full-time employment with law firms. If we want to keep comparing ourselves to other professions in terms of salary and image, it helps to act like other professionals in terms of gaining skills and putting in time.

Under-40 survey respondent Christine Kujawa, Head of Circulation Department/Reference Librarian, Bismarck Veterans Memorial Public Library, ND, explains: "I've seen many conversations going on about new LIS graduates who have no library experience complaining about not being able to find a job. As if getting the degree is their passport to employment. Young librarians should know that, if they have no experience, their job opportunities are much lower than graduates with library experience. They should be getting library experience while in graduate school. This isn't a new concept or something graduate schools should have to tell them. Law students work as clerks in law firms to get experience; medical students work as interns. Why should it be any different for our field?"

You can find more on job hunting in the next chapter, but it is never too early to start thinking about where you are going to take your degree and about building up your resume and acquiring desirable skills. Be proactive in looking for opportunities. Are area employers advertising pertinent internships that you can apply for now? These often do double duty, giving you academic credit as well as real-world experience; your school might also offer an internship program in which they will place you with a local employer. Take time to look at job ads while still in school, to see what employers are asking for—does your school offer coursework in these areas, or can you think of other ways to pick up skills that are often mentioned? Does your school offer a mandatory or voluntary practicum? Is there a nearby library where you might be able to volunteer? Can you pick up some committee work in your student association that will help build up your supervisory, budgetary, or technical skills? Can you apply for a part-time evening or weekend library position? Should you look into joining ALA/NMRT and/or your state association to see how these work and to start building a network of contacts? Most associations offer drastically reduced student rates to entice new members, so now is the time to experiment. Working while in school also allows you to experiment with different types of libraries or specialties to see what fits, as well as to meet professional colleagues who can act as references, mentors, and other sources of support.

Take some time to attend state or local conferences, which often offer reduced rates for students. Take some of the issues you are researching during library school, and work them into an article for publication. Participate on relevant e-mail lists; add substantive comments to the discussion rather than just asking questions. In their 2004 *Library Journal* article on "Fixing the First Job," Ria Newhouse and April Spisak point out that 26 percent of the new librarians they surveyed disagreed that their library science classes prepared them well and taught them skills they now use.[7] This means that a full quarter of the new librarians they talked to believe their schools failed to prepare them well for their jobs. In this case, how do we prepare ourselves? Those who are proactive from the beginning will find the field most welcoming post-graduation.

Going Back for the PhD

Although most librarians stop with the MLS (or with a subject-specialist master's degree; see Chapter 5), your career goals may eventually require additional education. This is particularly true if your grad school experience inspires you to want to teach other MLS students, if you are in a tenure-track position at a large research institution where a PhD would put you on more equal ground with other faculty, or if you eventually are aiming for the directorship of a large institution. One survey respondent in her 20s explains: "I plan on returning to graduate school within three years and pursuing a PhD, likely in library school or a related field. I think the changes that need to be made can only be made from within, especially within library schools. I want to teach the courses and skills that I think librarians of today need and make sure that young, bright graduates are motivated to be librarians."

Earning a PhD does open up different options, but also "overqualifies" you for many librarian positions; you may wish to have a specific goal and research topics in mind before deciding to pursue your doctorate—it is not a commitment to undertake lightly. Take time also to research the specific PhD you wish to earn, whether it be in library science, information science and technology, a subject-specific doctorate, or in a related discipline: What will make you most marketable, and what best matches your interests? As with the MLS, programs will vary widely in focus; some are more research- and philosophy-based, while others deliberately tie research to real-world issues.

As a younger librarian, you have the luxury of having plenty of time to work in the field and go back later to earn the doctorate. Any experience as an MLS librarian will make you more employable post-PhD. If your ultimate goal is to teach, practical MLS librarian experience will help keep you more in touch with the "real world." After some time in the field, those who go back for their PhD might find that the relationships they develop with their professors are stronger than those they developed during their MLS programs. First, returning students will be a bit older and, thus, more easily seen as future peers. Secondly, since nonadjunct LIS faculty generally have their own doctorates, the process of getting the PhD makes doctoral students part of their club in a way earning the MLS does not.

New forms of doctoral programs aim to address the shortage of incoming public library and school media specialists to teach a new generation of public library and school media students. The University of North Texas, for example, recently began offering an IMLS-funded experimental PhD program in library science that combines on-campus study with online and independent work. These types of PhDs are in their infancy, so this is a trend that may bear watching if you have interest in earning yours in the future. Be aware, though, of arguments that nontraditional programs lack the ability to enculturate doctoral students sufficiently into the academy, to allow for evaluation of their teaching abilities, to allow them to partake of related coursework from other departments, or to allow them to share research in-person with other students and professors. Such concerns may make it more difficult to find employment after earning a virtual—or partially virtual—doctorate than with an online MLS, especially if your goal is to teach in an LIS program.

Overall, librarians get from any graduate program—MLS or PhD—what they put into it. When you take the time to identify your goals and what you need to do to achieve them, you can maximize all of your educational experiences.

Endnotes

1. Derrick Jensen, *Walking On Water: Reading, Writing, and Revolution*, White River Junction, VT: Chelsea Green, 2004: 38.
2. Stephanie Maata, "Placements and Salaries 2003: Jobs! (Eventually)," *Library Journal* Oct. 15, 2004 <www.libraryjournal.com/article/CA471018> 26 January 2005.
3. John N. Berry III, "LIS Recruiting: Does It Make the Grade?" *Library Journal* May 1, 2003 <www.libraryjournal.com/article/CA292594> 17 March 2005.
4. Matt Wilcox, "Why I Won't Hire You," LISCareer.com, December 2004 <www.liscareer.com/wilcox_wonthire.htm> 26 January, 2005.
5. Tom Bahlinger, "Library Work Experience: Get Some!" in Priscilla Shontz, ed., *The Librarian's Career Guidebook*, Lanham, MD: Scarecrow, 2004: 140.
6. Barbara Lovato-Gassman, "Librarians in the 21st Century," in Karl Bridges, ed., *Expectations of Librarians in the 21st Century,* Westport, CT: Greenwood, 2003: 47.
7. Ria Newhouse and April Spisak, "Fixing the First Job: New Librarians Speak Out On Problems In the Profession," *Library Journal* August 2004: 44. (See also the sidebar interview with Ria Newhouse in Chapter 9.)

Surviving the Job Hunt

*Librarians are trained to find obscure information using complex
retrieval sources. While this work may seem routine at the reference desk, many librarians forget to apply this training when they
begin job-hunting.*

Laura Saunders[1]

ALA and other organizations continue to project a looming librarian shortage, especially at the management level, due to anticipated retirements over
the next 10 to 15 years. (See Chapter 1 for some statistics.) However, ever-
escalating reports of job cuts, the de-professionalization of positions, library
closures, and ever-increasing budget pressures seem to indicate otherwise—especially in the short term. As more and more new graduates enter a
tight entry-level market each year, the stress of the initial job hunt can cause
some NextGen librarians to harbor unproductive bitterness about the profession as a whole, toward professional associations, or toward those of their
colleagues who seem to be having an easier time gaining employment.
While this reaction is understandable, job-hunting NextGens need to learn to
separate their personal experiences from their outlook on the profession as
a whole.

Library Journal's (admittedly incomplete) annual "Placement and Salaries"
articles provide an interesting look at the job market for new grads over the
past few years. Each October 15 issue reports on placements of the previous year's grads, as of that spring. Although the number of respondents fluc-
tuates, given the schools and grads that choose to participate, their reports
seem to show a small but visible drop in the percentage of recent grads
reporting permanent professional employment between 2001 and 2004.[2] A
number of NextGens point out that those concerned about retention and
recruitment in order to ensure candidates for future vacancies should think

about the opportunities currently available to new grads, and how to keep them gainfully and professionally employed now. (See more on this in Chapter 10.)

The Job Hunt as a NextGen Issue

Several factors make job hunting a particularly relevant issue for NextGens. These include:

> ➤ The fact that most younger librarians are also new grads, many of whom are seeking entry-level positions in a currently tight market.

> ➤ The reality that next generation librarians face preconceived notions about their attitudes, work ethic, preparedness for the job market, and abilities that affect the hiring process. As Angelica Cortez, News Researcher, Fort Worth Star-Telegram, TX, says: "I wish I could say my age has no effect with the profession, but I feel it does. I think there is a very subtle, yet very real, apprehensiveness about hiring younger librarians." (Some older new grads also perceive ageism from employers reluctant to hire new librarians in their 50s and 60s; as with other job market factors, your mileage will vary.)

> ➤ The fact that younger librarians for whom this is a first career have less experience with the job-hunting process in general, leaving some unsure about what to expect or how to proceed.

> ➤ The concern some NextGen librarians have about the mismatch between their personal job-hunting experiences and the profession's current recruitment push.

> ➤ The truth that younger NextGens with less experience on the job market have had less time to build up references and to create the professional network that can make or break their job hunt.

While a successful job hunt can owe more to catching the right opportunity at the right time, having the right connections, or sheer persistence than to any magic formula, there are steps you can take both to maximize your odds and to ease the stress of the process. Most entail getting involved, getting connected, and giving back to the profession: You truly reap what you sow. What follows is a mixture of both general and NextGen-specific ideas for surviving the job hunt and increasing the odds of success, particularly during the hunt for that first entry-level position.

Where to Look

Many librarians job hunting in those parts of the U.S. close to library schools find that these areas tend to be glutted with new graduates, as well as with those with a couple of years of experience, seeking to move into desirable entry-level positions. Some newer librarians report being told that search committees receive upward of 100 resumes for decently paying entry-level positions in desirable locations or at prestigious institutions. Those students needing to support themselves, pay back student loans, and/or eat something other than Ramen noodles may find themselves holding out a long time for an entry-level job that meets both their salary and other expectations. If you are still in school, start your search six months or more before graduating; academic libraries, in particular, are notorious for taking months to complete a search, partially due to complex affirmative-action and EEO requirements. Be sure to state your projected date of graduation when applying, to show that you will have your degree in hand before starting a given job. Although the big picture is little comfort to those looking for entry-level positions, realizing that we are not the only profession to face a tight job market in a post-9/11, post-dot-bomb economy can help us retain some perspective.

It pays to understand the role that geography plays in your job hunt. Some states or urban areas seem more desirable to many, attracting more job seekers; some have two or more library schools churning out a new crop of grads each year; some face budget crises that affect funding for public libraries, school media centers, and higher education. Take cost of living into account when considering relocating; a salary that looks fantastic in Helena may not play well in Manhattan, especially when factoring in housing costs. Campuses with a library school sometimes refrain from hiring their own graduates, preferring to diversify the applicant pool—so, if you go to school in a town where your university is the major library employer, you may need to move post-graduation. Understand that most libraries will not pay travel

Online Resources for Job-Hunting Librarians

Librarians' job hunting now takes place primarily online, as employers realize the cost-savings of posting on the Internet and job seekers realize the time savings of searching and applying online. While the best resources for individuals will vary depending on your geographical location and area of specialty, there are a number of sites that will be useful to anyone. Realize that sites that merely mirror ads in print journals will be skewed toward upper-level positions for which institutions are willing to pay for ad insertion; local sites and those posting ads for free will be more inclusive.

➤ IFLA's LIBJOBS, infoserv.inist.fr/wwsympa.fcgi/arc/libjobs/
An international e-mail list devoted entirely to job postings for librarians and information professionals.

➤ Library Job Postings on the Internet, www.library jobpostings.org
Combined job postings with Lisjobs.com, plus links to many other job banks and library employment agencies.

➤ Lisjobs.com, www.lisjobs.com
Job postings are combined with those at Library Job Postings on the Internet (above); other resources include links to other job banks, advice and articles, and a resume-posting service. An RSS feed is available for new jobs.

➤ NMRT Resume Review Service, www.geocities.com/nmrtrrs/jobseekers.html
A free service for ALA/NMRT members; get feedback on your resume and/or cover letter via e-mail. NMRT membership is only $10 above regular ALA membership, which is well worth the price—and resume fodder in itself. (In-person resume

review at ALA Annual or Midwinter is free for members and nonmembers.)

Also subscribe to specialized e-mail lists in your area of interest, which often contain specialized postings. Supplement this by bookmarking job banks in your geographical location or area of specialty. Examples of these include:

➤ American Association of Law Libraries, Job Hotline, www.aallnet.org/hotline

➤ Michigan Library Association Jobline, www.mla.lib. mi.us/development/jobline.html

➤ Nebraska and Regional Library Jobs, www.nlc.state. ne.us/libjob/adjobs.html

➤ Society of American Archivists, Online Employment Bulletin, www.archivists.org/employment/index.asp

Find many more specialized and local job banks at http://lisjobs.com, as well as employment resources from library schools. Also look at online listings from specialized journals such as *The Chronicle of Higher Education* (chronicle.com/jobs/300/100/6000/), which also offers an RSS feed for its ads, and mainstream professional publications like *Library Journal* (http://jobs. libraryjournal.com) and *American Libraries* (www.ala. org/ala/education/empopps/careerleadsb/careerleads online.htm).

expenses for interviewees, especially for entry-level positions, as most cannot afford to do so. See if you can arrange a phone interview for the first round, or if they will otherwise accommodate distant applicants. Public libraries are often less "picky" about hiring entry-level new grads than are academic libraries, especially prestigious research institutions, but again, this varies from institution to institution.

If you are interested in academia, you might target smaller college libraries in your initial job search and get your foot in the door that way. While many librarians later move successfully between types of library or specialty, a number of institutions do place a premium on similar experience. Be aware of this if you have specific long-term career goals; beware of being pigeon-holed. (Other job-hunting assistance such as that from associations and conferences is covered in Chapter 7.)

How to Stand Out

To find gainful and relatively lucrative employment, you need to find ways to stand out among tens—or hundreds—of applicants. According to search committee veterans, this may not be as difficult as it seems. In a July 2004 NEWLIB-L post, for example, Eastern Illinois University (Charleston) Librarian and Associate Professor Sarah Johnson notes that around 80 percent of the resumes sent to search committees she served on in her previous position were never pursued further, for reasons varying from poorly written cover letters full of grammar or spelling errors, to cover letters that failed to target a specific position, to those that simply cut-and-pasted information from the ad without discussing how the applicant could meet these criteria.[3] Other hiring managers and search committee members report similar experiences; you need, first and foremost, to stay out of that easy-to-weed pile. You cannot guarantee yourself an interview every place you apply, but you can keep your application from missing that first cut every place you apply. When institutions know they will receive piles of resumes for a decently paying job in a popular area, they have the luxury of being more ruthless in their requirements and in weeding the stack of applications; you need to be more proactive in ensuring yours makes the cut.

Another problem new grads (especially younger new grads lacking library work experience) face is the perception by hiring committees that they are less prepared for their careers than were previous generations. A January 2005 letter to the editor of *Library Journal* even complains: "At my institution we have begun talking about the problem of the new graduates who have not been trained appropriately because we find we must take on more of the training! It feels as though the burden is being shifted to practitioners to provide much more library education than in the past."[4] Albany, NY, graduate student Teri Shiel notices: "I think that there is something of an unsaid age bias in this profession, something that I noticed on my first professional interview. Many comments were made about 'how young' I looked, and there was concern as to whether that would have any bearing on my capabilities as a supervisor. I feel that I was judged on appearance, rather than experience."

Work to overcome these perceptions by preparing yourself for tough interviews, acquiring relevant skills, and taking the time to show how you qualify for a given position. Hiring managers and search committees only have your application material to go by—you may be über-qualified for a given position, but how are they going to know if you fail to tell them? Making the effort to show what you bring to a given position is especially important when your experiences and expertise relate to, but do not exactly match, the list of required qualifications for the job: Be prepared to show how they qualify you. If you are switching specialties or types of library, show directly how your skills transfer; take the time to put them in language that will be familiar to those doing the hiring.

Showing your qualifications starts with writing your cover letter. Too many librarians—especially those looking for their first jobs—fail to take the time to tailor their cover letter to the specific positions they are applying for. They instead use a standard letter, and sometimes even forget to change the salutation! Too few let their personality and achievements shine through. Too few let potential employers know what they can do for their institution, and how their personality, skill set, and experience fit the bill. Too few take the time to research an employer, showing that they have spent time at the institution's Web site, browsing its collections, looking at its programs, or that they know what they have to offer that matches that library's specific needs. Too few make it clear that they want *this* job, they are excited about *this* institution, and not just out to take any job as a librarian. With all NextGens' talk about uniqueness, they need to live up to their own hype, and show how they stand out from other applicants. Remain focused and relevant and keep the emphasis on what you can do for an institution, on how you can meet the needs as stated in the job ad and/or additional descriptive materials.

Beyond simply paying attention to the basics and writing an effective resume and cover letter, younger librarians can stand out by tapping into their next generation energy and enthusiasm. When we have convinced ourselves that we are the right person for a job, we stand a much better chance of convincing others. When we believe in what we have to offer, we can convey that to hiring managers. When we believe in our own strengths and have a passion for a particular aspect of the field, we can let that excitement shine through. This is especially important in interviews, where energy and personality can go a long way toward making up for any lack (or perceived lack) of experience. Some sample interview questions and tips can be found online at www.lisjobs.com/advice.htm#interview; this issue also often comes up on discussion lists for new librarians. You can "practice" interviewing at local career fairs, or at ALA Annual or Midwinter or other conferences that offer placement services. Think in advance about questions you are likely to encounter, and have some stock answers prepared. Situational questions, for example, usually focus on qualities like leadership or problem-solving—think of an example of a previous situation where you have displayed each of these qualities, and be prepared to talk about it.

A big part of standing out involves cultivating the ability to translate any existing experience into library terms. Some younger librarians make the mistake of leaving previous nonlibrary jobs or school experience off their resumes, when in fact even the most basic retail, customer service, or management positions build many of the same skill sets needed by librarians. Emphasize in your cover letters and in interviews any experience dealing with the public, with difficult situations and people, with budgets or technology or marketing. Explain how the experience you have had student teaching, doing on-the-job training in a nonlibrary environment, or volunteer tutoring qualifies you to do bibliographic instruction or conduct public computer classes. Explain how the knowledge you gained in preparing a large class project, thesis, or paper relates directly to the requirements of a position. Show how your experience with one software package is comparable to experience with the one used at your target library; talk about how your committee work in any organization has built your teamwork skills. Show how your project management, event planning, supervisory, or other leadership experience transfers into an environment where many libraries are seeking leaders and mid-level supervisors and managers. In an academic interview, be prepared to talk about your future research interests, even if you are as yet unpublished; you can branch out here from work you did in library school or into an area of personal interest.

When helping patrons find information, we pretend expertise—or quickly acquire a veneer of it—all the time. This is a transferable skill; use it when boning up on an institution before your job interviews. Check out its Web site, read any application material a committee sends you, arrive early for interviews and take a walk around, and find out what you can from your network of contacts.

Keep in mind also that many libraries find themselves in desperate need of technologically savvy staff to serve ever-more demanding and tech-savvy patrons. Younger librarians who grew up with technology often have, or can assume, a natural comfort level with it. They can parlay that into positions if they are willing to play up their expertise—or their perceived expertise. Those who self-consciously reject the techno-stereotype and decide to embrace their inner Luddite should be aware that this will seldom be an advantage on the job market.

Look also at job descriptions and see where else your age can be an advantage: Does the position require working with teens? You are close to their issues, and may more easily relate to them, create programs for them, do collection development for them, and get to know them. Does the position involve readers advisory? Maybe you are a science fiction, or chick lit, or graphic novel aficionado, and can add personal expertise the library's current staff might lack. Look at your target library's existing programs and offerings, and come into an interview with ideas on how to expand these or create new ones. Libraries that do hire younger librarians often are looking specifically for an infusion of new blood and new ideas; why not capitalize on that need?

Be aware that you can often play up a combination of experience. Work part time? Count it toward the years of required experience for a position. Had an internship or an assistantship during grad school? That is, of course, experience. Add it in, call it "X years of experience," and broaden your search. Take the leap and apply for jobs you almost qualify for, even if you lack one or more items on an institution's lengthy list of requirements. Often these serve more as "wish lists" than as absolute requirements; libraries might also not be quite sure what they are looking for—until you tell them. Many tend to throw that laundry list out there to see what they get in response, so show them how the experience and skills you *do* have will serve them just as well.

Keep your resume or curriculum vitae (CV) current. An online portfolio works well for this purpose, as you can keep an ongoing record of projects, employment, professional development activities, and publications, and then pick out the pertinent bits to create targeted resumes when applying for positions. (For a nice summary of the differences between a resume and CV and a discussion of how to write and structure a CV, see ucblibraries. colorado.edu/internal/fac/V.D.5_cv.pdf.) Incidentally, forget the old "wisdom" of keeping your resume to a single page. If you are as professionally active as you should be, you will soon need two pages. Employers no longer expect resumes to be quite that brief, especially when so many are received electronically. Never remove important qualifications to make your resume fit on one page; never use a tiny font or mess with margins, which can make your resume (and you, by extension) seem cluttered and disorganized.

When you need to learn more about the types of positions available in libraries or about their specific duties, think about setting up informational interviews or tours with working librarians to get an idea of what their jobs actually entail. This allows you to more easily target your resume and interviews to specific types of positions.

Think carefully about who to use as references. Look for people who can give a realistic picture of your skills, strengths, and abilities, rather than for name recognition. You can use co-workers, professors, and mentors, especially if you do not wish to tell your current supervisor you are job hunting, or if this is your first library job hunt and you lack on-the-job references. This is another reason to build networks (see Chapter 7). Also be willing to serve as a reference for others as you progress in your career; give back, and keep the cycle going.

Starting Small

Be willing to start small and to be flexible in your requirements. Long-time librarians that complain about next generation librarians' unwillingness to "pay their dues" are right in one respect: Those who are willing to take less than desirable or less than well-paying entry-level positions gain that all-important experience for their resumes, are able to show supervisors their dedication, and often move up or on relatively quickly. Making sacrifices at the beginning can help you get your foot in the door; your first job—or second job—is not necessarily forever. Think about where you want to be in five years, rather than where you ideally want to be right now. As a next generation librarian, you have the time and luxury to do so.

Think about what you are willing to accept, and where you are willing to compromise. Is geographical location paramount? Is getting your foot in the door in a particular type of library a priority? What is more important to you: a good working environment or a high salary? What is the minimum salary you can live on? What is the minimum salary you can live on in a different geographical location? How important do you consider institution-supported professional development to be? Is it important to you to work with other younger librarians? Do you prefer a larger institution or a smaller one? Do you prefer more structure or less? Is having the opportunity for advancement/tenure/promotion/faculty status important, or are you planning to move to another institution after a couple of years anyway? Would you feel more comfortable working under a contract, or in an employment at-will environment? How do you feel about being part of a union?

Prioritize your list; there will always be tradeoffs. If salary is your main concern, for example, you may need to relocate, enter an area of librarianship that is of less personal interest, accept increased bureaucracy in a larger and richer institution, or investigate alternative careers. If gaining experience is your main concern, a small, rural library where you are expected to pitch in in every department may be a great resume and skill builder—with tradeoffs in terms of geography (depending on your preference) and salary. Thinking about these questions before and while applying can help you sort out the jobs appropriate to you. If your list of potential positions comes up empty, you are probably being too particular; look again and examine your priorities more carefully.

Be willing to apply for positions that are decidedly not your dream job; after a year or two, you can take your experience out the door and move on to more targeted opportunities. Look at these beginning positions as stepping stones along the way; start planning out your career path now. (Find more on planning career paths in Chapter 5.) Sheer odds mean that the more resumes you send out, the better your chances of landing an interview. New candidates in many fields need to take less desirable positions in order to get their foot in the door; we are not unique in this respect. New grads who burn to break into publishing, for example, often find creative ways to live in NYC on $22,000 per year—tripling up on roommates, waiting tables at night, or finding 50 recipes for economy-sized bags of rice. Many PhDs end up working three part-time adjunct positions to piece together a pitiful salary—despite what they were told a few years back about the potential in the academic job market, as long-tenured professors were supposed to begin to retire. Some end up moving up, and some end up choosing another career. But remember, you gain experience, wherever you start out.

Also, be willing to work part-time jobs at the beginning. This is obviously easier said than done, especially with the U.S. health-insurance coverage dilemma. Is it better, though, to work part-time in the field, or not to work in the field at all? Take one of these volunteer or part-time positions to gain experience, while also working at a full-time job with health benefits outside the field. Some libraries will hire pre-MLS part-time workers into librarian positions, with a salary bump upon completion of the degree, so look for these types of jobs even while you are still in school.

When applying for geographically remote positions, realize that most libraries will not pay relocation costs, and most will not even pay for travel to interviews. The larger and more well-funded the library, the better your odds, but this is still no guarantee. Hiring managers and search committees also can be suspicious of nonlocal candidates, wondering why you want to move, or why you are not able to find a job in your current area. Outline in your cover letter your reasons for relocating; the more specific, the better. If you are relocating, it is appropriate to ask about relocation assistance during your interview.

Another alternative is taking a temporary position or working with a library employment agency. If an employer, especially a larger institution, likes your work, they will most likely try to find a way to keep you on after the temp job ends (although, in cases where an agency charges a finder's fee for permanent placements, this may be a deterrent). If you are not hired on, though, you nonetheless have gained some experience for your resume and built up a bank of experiences to talk about on interviews. Some agencies will provide perks like health insurance to long-term or full-time employees; some do not, or instead specialize in temporary, short-term placements. Check with each for specific policies. Working with federal contractors, particularly, may offer you an "in" when it comes to applying for government positions in the future. You can find a list of agencies at www.lisjobs.com/temp.htm; realize that many do place people in several geographic locations, so it can pay to investigate even those outside your immediate region.

In some cases, taking a post-graduation paraprofessional position to gain experience can be appropriate. Libraries may even hire new grads for paraprofessional positions to get the benefit of their education without having to pay professional wages—which is a double-edged sword. While this can help you get your foot in the door, it can also contribute to the devaluing of the degree and alienate non-MLS paraprofessionals who are going through their own job search struggles. If you choose to go this route, be able to highlight the advantages your education and professional commitment can bring to the position. Working as a paraprofessional can show that you are dedicated to the field, and again, gives you fodder for future interviews and for your resume. Act as professionally as possible in any position, recognizing the importance of your work to the institution. Take advantage of professional development opportunities; keep active, even if you are not using all of your MLS skills in your particular job.

You do run the risk of being pigeonholed in parapro positions, or of being overburdened with tasks outside your specific job description and/or pay scale because your employer knows you have an MLS. Some employers are reluctant to hire grads in non-MLS positions because of a (probably justified) perception that they will leave for a higher-paying professional job at the first opportunity. Libraries, though, do often advertise professional or full-time positions internally before posting them to the outside world; a paraprofessional, part-time, or volunteer job can help you get your foot in the door.

Realize that new grads and less-experienced NextGens in many areas of the country are competing directly for positions with more experienced librarians with five or fewer years in the job market, many of whom are willing to move into desirable entry-level positions from their current entry-level positions in order to increase their current salary or potential for advancement. Emulate their strategy, and find a creative way to make that less desirable, lower paying entry-level job work so that you, too, can move on with experience under your belt. Once you have experience, you can also begin applying for the upper-level positions that libraries are having a hard time filling because of the lack of more experienced applicants (or of applicants willing to take on increased responsibilities). (For more on moving up, see Chapter 5.)

What to Watch Out For

Institutional environment is as important, if not more so, as a particular type of position, and you may have to try out more than one job to find your perfect fit. There are, however, some universally applicable warning signs that you should watch out for. Another reason to keep an eye on the job ads far out from actually applying for positions is to get a sense of who is advertising. Some institutions tend to advertise the same positions every few months, or to list an inordinate number of ads reading "search reopened." It is worth asking whether some libraries build up a deserved negative reputation due to the way they treat their applicants and/or existing staff. Long unexplained delays in responding to your application or getting back to you after an interview can also point to poor organization or excessive bureaucracy.

Interviews offer the opportunity for you to check out an institution's environment on its own turf. The pat advice is that, in an interview, you are interviewing an organization as much as they are interviewing you, ensuring the right fit for everyone. Do not be afraid to ask tough questions; do not be afraid to let your personality shine through. You can do this while remaining professional; committees and interviewers often welcome questions that show you have thought about their institution, can picture yourself working there, and are finding out what you need to know to succeed. If they do not enjoy the opportunity to talk about the institutional environment or library initiatives, this can be a warning sign in itself. Questions you may want to ask vary depending on the job and institution type, but can include queries such as:

➤ Why did the previous person leave the position?

➤ How is this corporate library funded?

➤ What type of relationship does it have with other departments?

➤ Who does this position report to?

➤ What kind of professional development and/or continuing education support does the institution offer? Does the library offer formal professional development or mentoring programs?

➤ How are professional reviews and evaluations conducted?

➤ What kind of cross-training opportunities does the library offer? How would you describe the interdepartmental cooperation in this institution?

➤ What can you tell me about the workplace culture and environment? What type of orientation does the library provide to new employees?

➤ What is your management philosophy or style?

➤ What kind of new projects or initiatives has the library been working on lately? (Alternatively, ask for details about specific initiatives you have seen announced in the literature, on their Web site, or that came up during the interview.)

➤ What challenges does the library currently face?

➤ Why does the library have so many job ads out at this particular moment?

➤ What goals do you have for the person filling this position? What do you see as its biggest challenges?

➤ What are some tenure requirements? How does the institution weigh scholarly activity and community involvement? What are the timelines, and what type of institutional support is offered? Do tenure requirements vary for librarians and teaching faculty? What percentage

of people typically achieve tenure? May I see a copy of
the institution's tenure and promotion document?

➤ Do librarians have faculty status? How would you
describe faculty/staff relations?

➤ What do you like best about working for this institution?

Ask a couple of questions along these lines, tailoring them to the job
and type of institution. Your pre-interview research can help you think of
other institution-specific ideas. Be careful, though, not to ask for information you were just given during the interview or that which is easily available online.

Be wary if, during or after an interview, you are not given opportunity
to speak to library staff (your potential new co-workers), are not given a
tour, or if all contact with staff members is closely supervised. Be wary if
you get a sense that there is a lack of communication, that your potential
colleagues dislike each other and/or their supervisor, or that they seem
to lack any enthusiasm for their work. Look for signs of negativity: Do
library staff seem to despise one another or their jobs? Look at staff work-
spaces; see if they are crowded together, if there are offices, and if the
institution, its collections, or its staff areas seem to be outgrowing their
space. Find out if there is a union; ask if the union agreement is online or
about what portions apply specifically to librarians. See if the job's
responsibilities are clearly laid out, either during the interview or in any
written material you are provided.

Look at the communication styles of the search committee and/or your
potential supervisor. If you are interviewed by multiple people, do they snipe
at each other? Is there a dead silence when an uncomfortable topic is
brought up? Do they seem to get along, or is there constant underlying tension? Do you get the sense that they are being honest with you? Do they
seem organized and on the same page with their questions?

Interviews will vary remarkably, depending on the type of institution and
position. Those at smaller public libraries may be quite informal and one-on-
one. Many academic institutions make their interviews into a drawn-out, two-
day affair involving multiple meals; you will likely be required to give a sample
presentation or instruction session. Large public libraries may require all
applicants to take a civil service exam, considering and interviewing only
those that come out with the top scores. Some institutions will extend a job
offer on the spot; others take weeks to decide among candidates.

Angie Brunk

Please summarize the story of your first professional library position and how it ended.

I began my position as the director of a small town library with a great deal of enthusiasm. Finally! I was putting all my skills, knowledge, and love of public service to use. My first morning on the job, the president of the board of trustees made a "joke" about firing me. I tried very hard to dismiss it as his quirky, and perhaps inappropriate, sense of humor. On some level, I knew something was very wrong, but I tried to dismiss it as part of getting used to a new place.

At the end of my first week, the president of the board met with me, and I could no longer ignore the warning signs. I had been told before I took the job that I would be evaluated every quarter, but now it was going to be "more often than that." The old director was supposed to remain for only a few days to make sure I could use the budgeting software, but now he was going to stay for the first month while the board decided whether or not I was going to work out. The board had not made any public announcement about the director retiring, in case things did not work out.

During this meeting, the president also said that the "over-55 set" had "strong opinions" about "college girls" and "kids these days." They did not approve of my lack of church attendance. They claimed my visual impairment was worse than I let on, and were concerned about "straining my eyes." I was also reminded repeatedly that they did not want any changes for at least six months.

It was quite obvious that the staff knew what was going on. One staff member, who was my subordinate, refused to hand over professional journals because I was only in the position for a "three month tryout." I was terminated with an hour's notice at the end of my third week on the job. It was quite obvious then that the staff knew before I did.

What part do you think that your age played in the situation? What other factors contributed?

I think my age played a significant role in the situation. My 25th birthday was also my second day on the job. Naiveté often comes with youth. I do not mean that in the sneering, condescending way it is often meant. However, there is no denying that, when facing my first professional position at the age of 25, I knew less than I do five years later. Had I been older, I probably would have been taken more seriously as a professional. With more professional experience, some of the warnings would have been impossible to ignore or interpret differently. With more experience, I would have known better how to stand up for myself. Age was not the only factor. I simply did not fit their vision of the person they wanted in my position. The person who took my place was also fresh out of library school and no more qualified, but was older, married, and had children. A young, single, and rather nontraditional woman was simply not the person they wanted as their library director.

What warning signs did you miss in the application/ interview process? What advice would you have for other next generation librarians looking for their first professional position?

Looking back, I know that I missed several warning signs. I had a gut feeling that this would not be a good fit for me. The president of the board did not sound enthusiastic when extending the job offer. In hindsight, the job offer seemed almost grudging. I was told that I would be evaluated quarterly, more often than usual, because I was so young. At least one of my mentors told me this could work to my advantage because I would be able to correct any problems quickly. I do not doubt that this is true in some circumstances. However, the fact that I was being singled out because of my age showed that the board was ambivalent, at best, about my appointment. The board was also very opposed to change, and said explicitly that they did not want to see any changes for six months. While I had no intention of going in to shake things up, it would be impossible for me to not change anything. I am not a clone of the person I was supposed to replace. The fact that a new person is in the position means that at least some change is inevitable.

There were several other warnings once I moved to the town and started the job. No one in town knew the director was even thinking of retiring, let alone that a replacement had been hired. I was introduced to only a few people while I was in the position. The people I met made it clear that they expected me to be just like the person I was replacing. The person I was replacing was in no hurry to teach me what I needed to know so he could retire.

What do you think was key in your getting past that first experience and finding the right fit?

I think it is important to recognize that something like this, especially if it is your first professional job, is not a small setback that can be easily overcome. Know that overcoming something like this will take time, patience, and persistence. The first thing you need to do is decide how you will handle this in your job search. Will you put it on resumes and applications? When I asked for advice, I received a great deal of very good, but conflicting advice. Most said there was no ethical reason I should list the experience. People were equally divided on whether or not I should list it for practical reasons. There is no one right answer in this case. Do what feels comfortable for you and be consistent. Know that you will always need to explain either the bad first job or the long job search in interviews. Know what your explanation is ahead of time.

Maybe I've read too many novels with blackmail plots, but I was not comfortable with hiding something. I tried leaving it off a few resumes, but it just didn't feel right to me. I will never know what really happened, but "the librarian I was supposed to replace decided not to retire" is a good enough explanation for interviews.

Anyone who tries to tell you luck does not play a role in the job hunt is kidding themselves. I went back to graduate school for my second master's, and found part-time library work to add to my resume. When I left school, I had stronger credentials, strong references, and the willingness to stick it out until I found the right fit. I endured a full year of job searching, and certainly went through periods where I wondered if I would ever find a job. After a year, I finally found an institution that was looking for someone with my skills and personality.

Is there anything else you'd like to share about your experience?

If you find yourself in a similar situation, accept the fact that it is unlikely you will ever fully understand what happened. I found the situation much easier to deal with and put in the past once I accepted that I will never have all the answers. I did consult a lawyer about a possible discrimination lawsuit. Unfortunately, because library directors serve at the pleasure of the board, they could legally dismiss me for almost any reason. Proving discrimination when I had been on the job only three weeks would have been next to impossible.

Aside from taking the miserable job in the first place, there are only two things I regret five years later. I did not seek professional counseling, but I should have. My friends, family, and mentors really pulled together to help me get through this crisis. However, I think objective, professional advice either from a career counselor or from a therapist would have helped me approach the job hunt with more confidence. While the termination was inevitable, I expected the timing to be different. I was caught unaware when the meeting actually occurred, and did not think to demand severance pay. I escaped with only one month's salary. In hindsight, I wish I had. I do not know if I would have succeeded had

> I tried to negotiate for more severance pay, but at least I would have stood up for myself.
>
> **Angie Brunk, 30, is Reference and Instruction Librarian at East Central University in Ada, OK.**

See the sidebar beginning on page 54 for an example of one younger librarian's negative first work experience. Most first jobs do play out less dramatically, but do watch out for warning signs and pay attention to your gut instincts, especially if you hit a desperate point in your job hunt. Again, define your priorities: Are you looking for high pay or happy co-workers? Geographical convenience or a well-run institution? If you have to ignore blatant warning signs and take a job just to get your foot in the door, be prepared to make an extra effort to separate your personal and professional life. Realize that institutional change is slow in coming, and you may need to just get what you need out of that job, and not hesitate to move on. Why show loyalty to an institution that shows none to you?

If you miss the warning signs and take an unhealthy job anyway, avoid beating yourself up about it. Some libraries, managers, search committees, and HR departments are very good at portraying themselves well in interviews and on paper, only later letting the truth about their personalities or working conditions emerge. Some libraries will deliberately misrepresent a position's responsibilities in order to get someone to take the job, or to get a candidate to take a complicated position for insufficient pay. Others may truly not have a clear idea what a job entails before offering it to you. (For more on surviving entry-level jobs, see Chapter 4.)

The job offer is also the place to begin salary negotiations. Some places are unable to negotiate because of union requirements, a budget squeeze, or rigid civil service or institutional pay ranges, while others, especially in corporate environments, may be willing or even expect to bargain. Once you are offered the position, you know that the institution recognizes your worth; some may actually expect negotiation on your part or respect you more if you take that initiative. Resources that may help you here are individual states' minimum salary guidelines for librarians, salary surveys, and an idea of typical ranges gleaned from colleagues or from watching the ads (salary surveys and related information are available at www.lisjobs.com/advice.htm#stats).

Look also at benefits—if you need to pay $200/month toward your own health insurance at one institution, but it is completely covered at another, you need to factor this in. Look at retirement benefits—yes, this seems a long way off at this point, but think about questions like: Can you roll benefits into another plan if you leave? Can you retire after 30 years of service in a given system, regardless of age? Also try to avoid falling into the trap of giving your salary requirements before interviewing; if you guess too low, they are not going to offer you more out of the goodness of their hearts. Let them know that salary is negotiable, and try to get the employer to mention a figure first.

Branching Out

In today's information-rich world, librarians' skills are overwhelmingly transferable to other fields and other institutions. Many schools prepare us for an overall information-management career in any setting; some, such as Berkeley, specifically go the information-management route and forego ALA accreditation. Look at related fields such as knowledge management, business intelligence, and becoming an independent information professional. At this point, many "alternative" careers are just careers; many younger information professionals may never want or expect to work in a traditional library. One survey respondent says: "I may go towards 'content' or 'knowledge' management, but I don't feel that this is leaving the field. I feel it is an extension of our field and I plan to do this, but may bridge the gap between the two concepts. This has been the failure of the Baby Boomer librarians—their inability and/or unwillingness to demonstrate their value to society and business in this concept shift; there should be *no* distinction … it should just be considered a continuum. So I don't consider myself to be leaving at this point … I've just started." Be able to understand and show how your skills transfer, and be careful to use the wording and jargon of your target industry.

Others can take heart in their ability to transfer their skills to other professions if the frustrations of a library job hunt or those inherent in many first jobs (or fifth jobs) sour them on the field. Give it a reasonable try, though, and avoid generalizing one bad experience and letting it sour you on the profession as a whole. Librarians have more options than in the past, and you can also consider working in an alternative field and then transferring your experience back to libraries. Beware, though, of spending too long outside of libraries if you plan to move back into the traditional field eventually; you can easily get stereotyped as a nonlibrarian. Make the effort to keep your traditional library skills fresh, especially if you are not using many of them in your alternative career.

Look also for alternatives in traditional libraries. A number of institutions offer post-graduate one- to two-year residency programs, aimed at introducing candidates to the world of academic librarianship and providing them with mentoring and other assistance. Most of these programs help residents develop a personal career development plan that will help guide them through their work lives as librarians. Residency programs generally seek highly motivated newer grads with potential to contribute to the field; you will want to show evidence of professional activity such as association involvement, committee work, volunteering, research, or publishing. Some public libraries also seek new grads for post-graduate one- or two-year internships, allowing them to learn the ropes by rotating through several different departments.

If you have been set on an academic or public library job from the outset, think about corporate librarianship, which often pays significantly better. The definition of "alternative" varies from person to person. You can also think of going out on your own, although this will be difficult if you have not yet built up some years of experience and contacts in the field. Vendors often employ those with library and technical, or library and training, experience—many pay better than traditional libraries, but you may need to be willing to travel or make other compromises.

Surviving Under- or Unemployment

Many new grads, especially those in areas glutted with library schools and their associated job seekers, face the unfortunate reality that it may take some time to secure that first—or second—full-time professional position. So, other than using your spare time to tweak your resume and troll the job sites, how do you keep busy? Hopeful? Professionally connected? Solvent? How will you keep your hard-won skills from atrophying?

Keeping productive during your job search helps keep you from being depressed, and any activities you undertake are potential resume fodder. Do you volunteer? Put it on there! Join one or more professional associations to make connections that will serve you during the job hunt and beyond; these often have reduced rates for unemployed librarians. (Find more on associations and conferences in Chapter 7.) You might consider taking a job in a bookstore or other related field while continuing your search; this will give you customer service experience and keep you tangentially connected to the profession. Need public speaking experience? Join Toastmasters or propose a poster session at a local conference; get other people together to form a panel, and propose a workshop.

While you are looking at the job ads, keep an ongoing list of the skills requested for those positions that interest you. How can you develop these skills? You have some time now—take a class, a workshop, or an online seminar. If you seem to be missing out on jobs of interest because they require certain common qualifications, figure out now how to get yourself those qualifications. Formal certificates, classes, or seminars are often a better choice than self-study, because you can list these on your resume and they serve as proof that you actually have taken the time to gain these skills. Evaluate your career goals and the types of libraries and positions that seem best for you. Keep reading—read online, read professional journals, read e-mail lists and blogs, and read popular literature.

Taking the time to keep professionally connected and involved is important on multiple levels. First, this gives you something to use to fill in those gaps on your resume. Second, it keeps you busy; you will have less time to obsess. Third, your professional activity helps keep a bad job-hunting experience from bleeding over into a frustration with the profession as a whole, which can easily affect your approach to future interviews and jobs. Fourth, it allows you to keep up with the profession. If someone asks your opinion in an interview on a current professional issue, you want to be current with your professional reading and able to form a coherent response. Be proactive from the beginning.

The same applies to surviving rejection; if you have ongoing professional connections and activities, you won't feel as if you are being rejected by the entire profession but by a single institution at a particular point in time. Try not to get your heart set on one "perfect" job; there will be many interesting opportunities and exciting options in your future, and rejection is just one institution's action at this particular time. You will never know the real reasons—maybe there was an internal candidate all along, maybe the final choice was between you and another person who seemed a hair better, or maybe the interviewer just didn't like your suit. Institutions are less than forthcoming about such reasoning in our litigation-happy society. Chalk it up to experience, and move on.

Endnotes

1. Laura Saunders, "Navigating a Tight Job Market: There's a Job For You," *C&RL News* 64:10 (November 2003): 661.

2. Salary survey results can be found in each year's October 15 issue of *Library Journal;* articles are available online. (Go to www.libraryjournal.com and do a search for "placements and salaries"—this results in additional results, but the last few years of these October articles will be listed.) Realize that a number of MLS programs decline to participate, and, of those who do, not all grads respond.

3. Sarah L. Johnson, post to NEWLIB-L e-mail discussion list, 22 July 2004. Quoted with permission.

4. Peggy Daub, letter to the editor, *Library Journal* Jan. 15, 2005, www.library journal.com/article/CA491136, 24 January 2005.

4

Surviving Entry-Level Positions

The actions you take during your first three months in a new job will largely determine whether you succeed or fail. Transitions are periods of opportunity, a chance to start afresh and to make needed changes in an organization. But they are also periods of acute vulnerability, because you lack established working relationships and a detailed understanding of your new role.

Michael Watkins[1]

As you begin your career as a librarian, you will move on to new concerns. How do you survive—and thrive—in a workplace dominated by professionals much older than yourself, or in one that seems overly bureaucratic or resistant to change? How do you keep professionally active and involved, particularly in cases where your workplace offers little institutional support? How will you distinguish yourself in an entry-level position, and develop the skills you need to move up or on? How will you begin planning out your career? How can you supplement or stretch out a low entry-level salary? Most NextGens put a lot of effort and time into their job hunt; now, resist the temptation to relax calmly into your new position. You have worked up some momentum—keep going! You have the excitement of getting the job offer—hold onto that excitement!

Any new position requires a period of adjustment. The way in which you settle into your first or any entry-level position, though, is especially important. These jobs serve as your introduction, not only to one particular workplace, but to the profession as a whole. The previous chapter talked about interviews as a way for both parties to evaluate the other. When you begin your first entry-level library job, you will soon realize the importance of choosing carefully and will find out whether you have located the right fit—and your library will see if it has found the right fit in you. Your first few months, in some respects, are an extension of this mutual evaluation process. Over time, the honeymoon period will end and you will each see what the other is really like. The following sections talk about the transition process and how to settle into and excel in a new position. While the focus is particularly on first or entry-level positions, much of this discussion also translates into settling into any new job.

Surviving Entry-Level Jobs as a NextGen Issue

What makes surviving entry-level positions a NextGen issue—other than the obvious point that many younger librarians are currently in, or entering into, their first or second professional positions?

> ➤ First, many NextGens are new to the job market in general. For some, especially for Millennials who went straight from college into an MLS program, their first entry-level library position is their first "real" job, which requires an associated shift in priorities, expectations, and attitude.

> ➤ NextGen librarians encounter perceptions and stereotypes from co-workers and patrons that affect their ability to settle in or to distinguish themselves in their entry-level jobs; they need to learn how to deal effectively with these perceptions. Anthony Auston, Librarian, Homewood Public Library, IL, notes: "It's true that many of our senior staff members are old enough to be our parents—in fact, I imagine that they must have children our age. One obstacle we may face is being treated as children of our seniors, rather than colleagues, equals, or the future leaders of the library."

> ➤ Younger librarians have many years ahead of them in the profession. What they do at the outset of their careers can set the tone for their future, and determine where they go from there.

> ➤ Entry-level jobs are the place to begin developing the skills, experience, and attitude that allow NextGens to be taken seriously in the workplace and by future interviewers and employers.

➤ Next generation librarians are entering a changing profession, which sometimes can cause them to be viewed as a threat by their more established colleagues who see them as representative of this change. Alex Brown, Liaison Librarian, University of Western Sydney, Australia, says: "It should be noted that, while new librarians have skills and knowledge and are slightly better at adapting to the changing information and work environments, the institutions that they work for are still managed by the 'older' generation of librarians who may be finding it hard to adapt and understand themselves, and this can facilitate feelings of fear and insecurity. The older librarians can also see the structures and organization of the information environment quite literally 'crumbling' around them, being replaced by an environment that is quite fluid and lacking the tight composition they are used to. This can provoke a reactionary response."

➤ NextGens are often taken aback by their institutions', co-workers', and administrations' resistance to change, and find that they need to deal with the contrast between their initial expectations and long-standing institutional traditions. One survey respondent echoes many in saying: "It is highly surprising to me how stuffy and slow-moving my library is in making decisions and making things happen. My experience in library school was so engaging and eye-opening. I felt like I was working on the cutting edge of technology. Now that I'm actually working in a library, my colleagues are less excited about technology than I am and I often feel alone in trying to implement new technologies." Another says: "I was told I was hired because I had all the new knowledge from library school and working at the large university library. When I propose to make changes based on this knowledge, I get tons of resistance from my director, who is in his 30s, but went to library school when the Internet was considered junk and most reference sources were still easier to access in print (10 or so years ago)."

> ➤ NextGens need to develop a mutual respect with their colleagues of all ages, and on their first jobs they must learn to act and work as library professionals.

> ➤ Those right out of school may have been exposed to cutting-edge technology and innovations during their graduate programs, but may end up in libraries with little funding to implement these types of technologies and programs or that are slow to adapt to change. This can require a shift in expectations and cultivation of patience.

Any entry-level position allows you to begin building the experience to move forward, or to move on. Even a cursory examination of current library-related job ads shows that many either prefer or require some professional-level or library-specific experience. Even in a less than ideal workplace, take heart in the thought that you are expanding your future employment prospects and adding to your resume.

Your Responsibilities

Younger librarians in entry-level positions, particularly those in their first "real" job, may tend to place all of their expectations on their institution and supervisor without also taking the initiative to settle smoothly into a new position. No one, though, is more responsible for moving forward and for settling effectively into the job than you are. The first job, especially, provides a fantastic clean slate, which brings tremendous opportunity, but also tremendous responsibility. Make sure that you have a copy of your job description, learn its ins and outs, and then begin assimilating the unwritten expectations of your position. Fill the responsibilities of your specific job before beginning to stretch beyond, realizing you will likely be reviewed within three to six months (which is often a probationary period). Act on any feedback you are given; arguing about it is usually less than productive. If you feel that expectations are unfair or that you are being perceived as less competent largely due to your age, work on changing these perceptions— or on moving on.

Realize that no one generally hands out leadership or professional development opportunities; you will need to seek them out or find a way to develop your own. As Roy Tennant writes: "Your place of employment owes you the time and training to do the tasks at hand, unless you were hired because of specific knowledge and skills. Beyond the requirements of the job, you must heed your calling as a librarian and information professional. To be effective in our profession you must constantly learn and retool."[2]

Many next generation librarians find that library school did not fully prepare them for their jobs. Rebecca Rankin, Adult Services Librarian, Northlake Public Library District, IL, says: "Boy, they really kid you in library school when they talk about job interviews and starting a new job. I have had to teach myself most everything at both jobs I've started post-MLS graduation. There is a huge disconnect there. Employers expect you to have learned skills in library school that they know you didn't learn, because they themselves did not learn these skills in library school. Library schools tell graduating students employers will train them, but they don't really know that, because faculty haven't worked in libraries in eons, if ever." Be a self-starter, and fill in those gaps for yourself. As Jill Emery writes: "... you will appreciate your job and your new work environment more if you invest time to learn about it a bit more and to take some initiative to comprehend the bigger picture. More often than not in library and information science programs, what you are asked to do is be a rule follower. You are told what to look at, when to look at it, and how you should present it back in your classes for a grade. Out in the workday world, however, you are often left to direct the project you are given and to take the initiative to understand and comprehend complex organizations and their interoperability ... The more of a self-starter you are, the further along you will be when your first evaluation rolls around or when the first opportunity for promotion presents itself."[3]

Take the time to learn your specific institutional environment and workplace culture. Every library has its own. If you try to make changes too quickly or act without knowing the pertinent personalities, rituals, and norms, you can inadvertently step on people's toes or engender reflexive resistance. This is true whether your first position is as one of 20 reference librarians in a huge institution or as the director of a small rural library. Janet Crum, Head, Library Systems & Cataloging, Oregon Health & Science University, Portland, recognizes the importance of balancing the desire to effect change with respect for tradition—as well as the need for patience: "I have experienced this phenomenon from both sides—as a brash newcomer full of ideas and impatient with entrenched bureaucracy, and as a semi-veteran who has had to explain and justify current procedures to newcomers. Based on my experience, I'd like to encourage those already in the profession to carefully consider the ideas and suggestions of the young newcomers. Very often, they can see things you cannot, because they don't have an emotional investment in the status quo. Your library cannot grow if you don't step out of your comfort zone and try something new once in awhile. To the newcomers, I recommend patience. When I first took my position, many of my ideas got shot down, and I became demoralized. Over the course of a few years, though, I saw many of those ideas implemented. People needed time to get used to the new ideas and see the need for themselves. You can't expect to change old habits overnight." Settle in and take the time to find out your responsibilities; never be afraid to admit where and when you need guidance. Seek out mentors, both inside and outside of your workplace, and get to know your colleagues as people—which will also let you learn who holds both official and unofficial power in your institution.

In a tenure-track environment, one of your first responsibilities is to find out institutional expectations of tenure-track librarians. How heavily does your institution weigh scholarship, campus and community involvement, peer-reviewed vs. non-peer-reviewed publication, prestigious vs. more general journals? Do conference presentations or poster sessions count toward tenure requirements? Does association or in-house committee work impact tenure decisions? Does your library offer mentoring or peer group support? Does it offer release time for research? Are there periodic reviews or evaluations along the way, and what is the tenure timeline? Realize that, in many institutions, those who fail to achieve tenure will not have their contracts renewed and will find themselves seeking alternate employment; take the process seriously from the beginning.

GenX librarians with a few years in the profession express some different ideas on the concept of "paying dues." Some working library experience can provide a different viewpoint, or this may reflect a difference between the outlooks of Generation X and Generation Y in general. Again, many mention the feeling of being "in between," able to understand both the concerns of younger librarians who want to jump in and hit the ground running and of older professionals who emphasize the importance of taking the time to learn the ropes and gain experience. As Chrissie Anderson Peters, Librarian, Basler Library, Northeast State Community College, Blountville, TN, explains:

> I honestly feel like I'm somewhere in the middle of most issues in the profession right now, as far as age is concerned. I can see both sides of most arguments, but must admit that I get terribly frustrated when I read thread after thread after

thread on lists such as NEWLIB-L, where so many newer librarians and/or students seem to do nothing but moan and complain about the job situation. (There are times when I have to remember to be professional and not just send out a response telling these persons that their attitude might have more to do with it than the lack of experience or lies they think they've been told by library school recruiters!) I believe that nothing in life worth having comes without a cost and without effort—sometimes I'm not so sure that a majority of the "new" librarians really "get" that. On the other hand, I see librarians who have been in the profession for 10 plus years, who have such a chip on their shoulders about letting younger librarians into their inner circles, that I just want to say: "Hey, if you really care about the profession, let them in—show them the ropes, help them to understand why you do things the way you do them, help them appreciate where the profession has come from so they can help it continue to grow and attract intelligent and dedicated people." If those of us in leadership positions don't accept younger librarians in and learn from them and with them, then we're going to have a terribly dysfunctional profession in the next five to 10 years, I'm afraid.

As with any issue worth talking about, this one has at least two sides—and NextGens who work to gain experience can sometimes find that with time they both earn the respect of, and find mentors in, their older and/or more experienced peers.

Dealing with Dinosaurs

"Dinosaur" here does not connote age, but attitude. Surveyed NextGen librarians in their first positions were often quite surprised by their institutions', administrations', or co-workers' resistance to change. Leslie Bussert, Reference & Instruction/Ethics & Humanities Librarian, University of Washington, Bothell, for one, says her biggest surprise "would be my drive for tackling new ideas/projects/services and how they were met with attitudes from management like, 'well, that's not how we do things here …' or, 'we don't have money for that' or, 'we don't have the time/staff for that.' Some ideas I presented were not even that 'big' of projects—just ideas I felt worth pursuing or that would help put us in the direction other libraries are going towards innovation or technologies. They wouldn't have required much funding or staffing, and being the one to present the idea, I was also willing to be the one to spearhead the projects and even willing to work on them myself." Melissa Rabey, Teen Librarian, Brandywine Hundred Library, Wilmington, DE, shares similar concerns: "As a younger librarian, I have a lot of new ideas, but often originality of thought is frowned upon. I've found that I keep coming up against a mentality of 'we tried that 10 years ago and it didn't work—why should we try it again?' Or, even worse, I see an attitude of 'but we've always done it like this!' Being younger than many of my colleagues, it can be difficult to press for new programs and ideas."

I have a preschooler at home, so I am subjected to more than my fair share of children's TV. While we were immersed in a recent episode of *Sesame Street* on the theme of dealing with change (Big Bird, distraught that the shopkeeper was going on vacation, wondered who would make his birdseed milk shakes the way he always likes them), it occurred to me that the fear of change is not the exclusive territory of older workers; we all need stability in one form or another. (It also occurred to me that *Sesame Street* is no more heavy-handed than change-management titles purportedly aimed at adults, such as *Who Moved My Cheese?*)

Some non-next generation librarians' fear of change might be focused more closely on dealing with technology, moving into retirement, or making midlife career shifts, while younger librarians' fears might be focused on making the transition from academia to that first real job, moving into management, or untangling the tenure or promotion process. Either way, all librarians should be able to empathize with each other's concerns and understand our common need to build on some foundation of stability.

Next generation survey respondents overwhelmingly mentioned their colleagues' fear of change as a disappointing factor as they entered the profession. Some opined that this was due to their co-workers' ages, while others just encountered layers of bureaucracy that their institutions had built up over time. Christina Stoll, Knowledge Management Specialist, North Suburban Library System, Wheeling, IL, explains: "I think my age plays a part in that I grew up as the current technological advances were happening, so I'm more comfortable with rapid change." Another respondent says that: "… the amount of hierarchy, politics, and inefficiency took me by surprise. Librarians are intelligent enough to find better ways of doing things than tiptoeing around the boss, wheedling and cajoling for necessary things, holding useless meetings, feeling fear and hopelessness about things ever changing …"

Some under-40 survey respondents view change resistance as a function of long-time librarians' burnout and career stagnation, rather than of age per se. "I think that I could be seen as a threat to established librarians who do not have open minds. Many of my friends from library school were 45-plus, and I think that they can handle working with people of all ages. Librarians who have been in their jobs for a while do not seem as open to new ideas and new people." Another Millennial respondent concurs: "I am often frustrated with older colleagues who have been around for 20, 30, 40, or more years—they are often cranky, and burned out from serving the public and keeping up with technology. Every exchange with a patron is an opportunity to show what we can do, the resources we have, and to make library users out of everyone. They refuse to do more than is necessary in order to get the patron to go away." Others mention concerns about some colleagues nearing retirement who seem unwilling to rock the boat at this point in their careers: "Younger librarians are more willing to change and adapt; older, more established professionals often want to maintain the status quo. (I've heard some say that they want to maintain this—at least until their retirement in the next few years.)"

Whatever the reasons, NextGens' understanding that libraries and librarians need to adapt in a time of rapid change needs to lead them to become change agents within their institutions, to help invigorate their libraries by providing new viewpoints and the willingness to question the status quo. There are a number of ways to go about this; those with less likelihood of alienating colleagues stand the best chance of success. Cultivate the ability to balance the need for change with respect for institutional memory and strengths, which can be frustrating in libraries where some colleagues want nothing to do with the process. One survey respondent writes: "I was the youngest person at the library when I was hired. I sometimes feel that I'm constantly banging my head up against the stodgy, stuck-in-the-past librarians who are resistant to change, regardless of their age. I also feel that I'm missing the history and culture of the institution, and that it is very difficult to keep the history and facilitate change in a positive manner."

NextGens need to retain a respect for institutional history and for the skills and knowledge of all of their colleagues. As one under-40 survey respondent notes, "I also think that sometimes some new librarians think they know everything right out of school. I think that is the wrong attitude. Even with 10 years of experience, we still have a long way to go before we have 25 or 30, and we should not forget to learn from others. What is the point in destroying relationships, and then having to reinvent the wheel, instead of taking the wheel and just tweaking it a little?" The first few months—or year—on a job, can provide time to settle in. Once in the full swing of things, you may find you have more projects than you can handle. Balance your desire for each change with an understanding of how it affects everyone and fits into the organizational culture. Emphasize one idea at a time, follow through on your projects, and resist the urge to try and change everything at once.

Over-40 survey respondents have some pointed advice along these lines for their younger colleagues. One says: "Be respectful of your elders. I know that it is frustrating to see situations that you can remedy with your brilliant education, and be thwarted with naysayers and those who claim that we don't have the time or money, but library workplaces are full of egos and politics, and it pays (in the long run) to be kind and respectful. I've seen brilliant people get ignored when a job opportunity came up because they were so obnoxious with their presentation of their 'better' ideas." Tina Hubert, General Consultant, Lewis & Clark Library System, Edwardsville, IL, concurs: "Change things while honoring the past. I'd like to emphasize the need to honor the past ... it is hurtful to 'seasoned' librarians to have newer librarians come in and change all of their years of hard work. [Show] that the next generation understands that, without the groundwork laid by the older librarians, the library profession wouldn't be poised and ready for the next generation. That's not to say that the responsibility is only on the next generation, but it is in the next generation's best interest to consider how they approach different issues, in order to pave the way for new ideas in the best possible manner." Nora Fitzgerald Hardy, Assistant Director and Manager of Council Programs, South Central Regional Library Council, Ithaca, NY, suggests: "Do not be easily discouraged from workplace solutions which you develop —tradition can keep older/more conservative professionals from accepting change easily. Conversely, do solicit input from senior/older staff members who can provide long-term perspectives and institutional 'memory.' Sometimes there *are* good reasons for not doing something, or doing it slowly."

Understanding these perspectives can help you get yourself and your ideas taken seriously by long-term colleagues and administrators. As Geoffrey Bellman points out: "We do a great job spouting off about how things ought to be and the big changes that are needed. In the process we often succeed in alienating many people who worked very hard to bring the organization to where it is today. While we are spouting, do we recognize that we will need the help of these slightly resentful people who are listening to us? Do we recognize how our proposals sound to them? Do we care?"[4]

Part of looking at generational differences also involves recognizing where each generation tends to have its strengths, and acknowledging that the profession is stronger for combining those strengths. Elaine Hagen, Part-Time Reference Librarian, Bethel Park Public Library, PA, shares: "I think a staff with a wide range of ages is a good staff. We are each able to identify with different patron groups. I am able to share what I have recently learned in library school. I share the 'hot topics' and new ideas. My more experienced colleagues are able to share more practical information, such as how to handle problem situations." One over-40 survey respondent also finds intergenerational interaction fruitful: "I find the younger librarians tend to push the limit on rules, service guidelines, etc., which in turn makes me rethink how or why we do things. I rein them in a bit, and they make me think outside the box. Sometimes I'm amazed that they have the influence to make me more flexible."

NextGens' Singular Strengths

How do younger librarians capitalize on their unique strengths? One NextGen says: "I am enthusiastic, eager to try new things, face new (and old) challenges—I think this is a reflection of many young librarians—we're excited to change the world! And if not the world, at least our libraries." NextGens in workplaces that recognize the need to blend multiple viewpoints and perspectives are able to bring fresh insights and feel that their unique contributions are valued. Another NextGen respondent says: "The Boomer colleagues I work with here view me more as having a 'fresh perspective.' They count on me and the other younger librarians here to see things differently than they, who are looking through a lens of 10 to 25 years of experience, see them."

Realize that your age affects your co-workers' and the public's perceptions, but that it is also possible to turn these perceptions into a strength—especially when dealing with students or other younger patrons. Under-40 respondents noted:

> ➤ "Being in an academic setting, I feel like my age helps younger students relate to me. I feel like I may have a better understanding of the way our students grew up surrounded by information and technology."

➤ "I feel that being my age is a plus in the particular job I do. I'm still young enough, in my opinion, for the teens to relate to, and old enough to be considered a 'trusted adult.' "

➤ "I think that my youth can be useful. I'm less intimidating for younger patrons. The students I supervise seem to identify with me, which makes our working relationship better. I'm also able to empathize with them, so I know how to avoid pushing them too hard."

➤ "As a librarian at an undergraduate library, my age also allows me to better understand how today's generation of traditionally aged (18–22) undergraduates approach research."

Find more on generational perceptions in Chapter 6.

One of the most prevalent images of next generation librarians includes the perception that they have an innate facility with technology. Whether this is true of all NextGens or not, the very perception means that many younger librarians will be on the forefront of dealing with technological change, or will be expected by their institutions and co-workers to be the ones to handle technological problems. (Find more on the relationship between younger librarians and technology in Chapter 9.)

NextGens' Expectations

Many younger librarians were told when applying to library school or when researching librarianship as a career that there was to be an imminent wave of retirements that required NextGens' immediate input and employment. Many, though, have found this less than true on the job—or, as mentioned in Chapter 1, that the timetable for these expected waves of open positions keeps being pushed back. As Amy Phillips, Reference Librarian, Philip S. Miller Library, Douglas County Libraries, Castle Rock, CO, notes: "When I entered the field, I was told there would be a rapid changing of the guard which would allow us to move into leadership rapidly. My perception is this bill of sale was incorrect, so how will we handle a professional setting where we may be the junior librarians for the next five to 10 years?" NextGens need to adjust their expectations to longer entry-level periods or to institutions that do not want them yet to act as leaders, incorporating the understanding that change is a process. Younger librarians need to find ways to adapt to bosses' and/or co-workers' differing communication styles, paying attention to both generational and general differences.

The biggest transition for most entry-level librarians, whatever their age, involves adapting to a long-standing organizational culture. This encompasses everything from an informal understanding about who takes which parking space, to preferred channels of communication, to policies and procedures so old that no one remembers their actual origins. While many institutions bring in "new blood" precisely with the expectation of shaking up existing organizational culture, some most definitely do not. You will quickly be able to ascertain your administration's—and co-workers'—preferences. You also need to take the time to understand your particular organization's culture before you know what might need changing and what is worth honoring. Most importantly, you need to get to know the various personalities in your institution and how they interact, how open they are to change, and how territorial different departments seem to be. Do not expect to go into most entry-level positions and have an immediate opportunity to change the way things have always been done. Pay attention for a while; learn who is approachable and where to build support.

As an MLS student, you may have had the opportunity to deal with cutting-edge technology and to read about or participate in innovative programs. In reality, many libraries lack the funding, know-how, or political will to implement much of this. In this situation, think of concrete ways you can help move your library forward—and about what best serves the needs of your patrons. There are often major hurdles to cross before getting to new and cool, especially when it comes to technology. Get the basics down first, think of logical steps to take, and match your expectations to what is reasonable for your institution.

Another common NextGen concern involves a lack of challenges in entry-level positions. Beyond the challenge of matching graduate school to real-world expectations, others find that their positions are far enough down the ladder to be less officially involved; many entry-level positions emphasize rote tasks and work. So, if you are not challenged by the duties of your first job, how do you go about making your own challenges? Volunteer to help with projects, look at what needs doing and take responsibility on your own. Join institutional committees; read the professional literature and get on the routing lists for key publications to which your library subscribes. Be a problem-solver—use your fresh perspective to offer ideas and constructive solutions. See if your library offers cross-training opportunities, so that you can gain experience in multiple departments and skills in various areas. Keep an ongoing record of the projects you take on and accomplish. This is fodder for your next job hunt or when negotiating a raise or promotion. Create a portfolio and keep it up-to-date; be prepared to talk yourself up.

In an academic environment, you may also find that as a newer librarian you will be volunteered for committees and other ongoing projects. This is one part of "paying your dues." Learn when you can and cannot say no, and when it may be required or politically expedient to participate, even if a given committee seems on its surface uninteresting. Learn what projects are good career-building experiences, and what will look best on your resume or tenure/promotion document. Look for fringe benefits, like getting better connected to the larger campus, finding out ways to serve student subgroups, or having an impact on tenure or promotion guidelines. Gain experience with budgeting, leading teams, or completing projects. The more directly a committee or project relates to your present job or career goals, the more valuable it will be.

Others' Perceptions

Many NextGen librarians report reluctance by both staff and patrons to take them seriously as professionals. Younger librarians who staff reference desks, for example, often hear questions from patrons such as: "Where's the real librarian?", "Are you a student?", or "Do you work here?" Annie Bergeron, Librarian, Bloom Trail High School, Chicago Heights, IL, says: "Students will often ask me where the librarian is, even though I may be in my office that is clearly labeled 'Librarian.' I think that many do not have faith that I can really know enough to be able to help them. I have surprised many!"

Surprising patrons by providing effective services is in itself the best way to combat negative perceptions. Twist this positively—by sitting at that desk, managing others, or just carrying out your job duties efficiently and enthusiastically, you are providing an image of a librarian that other younger people can relate to. Your presence and professionalism allow them to think of "librarian" as a career possibility, and can in itself help overcome some people's reluctance to approach their local librarians for assistance. (For more on image and overcoming such perceptions, see Chapter 6.) Further, realize that different groups of patrons may be comfortable with different staff members: Some may prefer to deal with your older colleagues; some may prefer to deal with you; some may prefer to deal with a woman or a man or someone who looks more like them; or some may prefer to deal with someone they have talked to before. Some may prefer, consciously or unconsciously, to address different types of questions to different types of staff members on the assumption that you will know different things, or will react differently to the question itself. You cannot control people's impressions; all you can control are your reactions to them.

NextGen librarians who enter librarianship as a second career or who have a few years in the profession sometimes relate to patrons somewhat differently, which can be another distinction between GenX and GenY librarians. Kevin Moore, an MLS student from Portland, OR, notes: "At 35 I am entering my second career, so I bring to it experience from 'the real world' that I didn't have when I was an undergrad. Most significantly, I have tried various other avenues—jobs, projects, self-employment, another career—and have met with a mixture of failure and success. This prepares me well for dealing with patrons who may be undergoing similar transitions wrought by our volatile global economic conditions."

Some of those who are the first younger librarians for years to enter workplaces dominated by older, long-term library professionals report an excess of solicitude by co-workers unsure how to interact with a colleague young enough to be their child—or grandchild. (If you end up managing these types of workers, see more on moving into management in Chapter 5.) Others in this situation find that some of their co-workers tend to minimize their contributions, or expect them simply to be seen, not heard. Many librarians and library workers place an overwhelming primacy on library experience, especially experience in their own institution. They may worry about what you might do to what they have spent years building up. Martin Garnar, Reference Librarian, Dayton Memorial Library, Regis University, Denver, CO, says: "I think that we are causing the profession to hunker down and look for ways to protect the edifice they have built, as if we're prepared to come in and tear everything down just because we have questions about how things are done. Our healthy disregard for tradition lets us think of new ideas, but we won't summarily dismiss all that has come before."

Many younger librarians mentioned the need to prove themselves in their entry-level positions, and the fact that it took some time to overcome people's initial stereotypes. One notes: "I think that you have to prove yourself a lot more when you are young. I was the youngest in my class and the youngest at my library. There is a lack of confidence in our abilities simply because we are young." Another concurs: "Most important, I think, is the *perception* of NextGens as a generation apart. We are supposed to bring innovation and tackle new challenges, but we must also mind our elders and avoid stepping on anyone's toes." Martin Garnar continues by saying: "I have to constantly prove my worth, as I feel like I'm not as respected because I haven't been a librarian for 30 years."

How do you go about proving your worth? Instead of using your energy to complain about a lack of respect, earn that respect by bringing solutions. Complaints seldom lead to respect, but constructive criticism and positive ideas can. Learn the organizational culture and work within it to achieve your goals; be able to back up your ideas, and realize that you will build credibility over time. Just as you often need to start small in the job search process, you can prove yourself here on smaller projects before proposing library-changing initiatives. Building a successful track record proves that you are worthy of trust and increasing responsibility. Kam McHugh, Randolph Branch Manager, Memphis/Shelby County Public Library & Information Center, Memphis, TN, explains: "... it has been my experience that most people in the library profession overlook age when someone has proved their capabilities. I've worked very hard in my short career, and I think my older supervisors and colleagues respect what I do, regardless of my age. No one has ever been jealous of the advances I've made in my career at a young age; I've proven my capabilities." Demonstrate your respect for their contributions as well.

If you are in an entry-level librarian position, require that your colleagues treat you as a professional. If, in a bid for initial acceptance, you try to be overly helpful in ways unrelated to your job—making their copies, making their coffee, and doing their busywork—you are letting them treat you differently than other co-workers because of your lack of experience and your age. They then have an "in" to continue to walk over you in other areas. Be polite and be professional, yet be firm in that you are a professional colleague. The "other duties as assigned" clause in most job descriptions does create a gray area, but when an institution pays you as a professional, it is a waste of their investment if you spend your time doing others' clerical or busy work. There is a fine line here—you do have the responsibility to work as part of a team and contribute your time and effort to group projects, but this does not extend to taking on others' duties that take away from the professional work you need to be doing.

Be aware also of the ways that age can affect workplace bonding and socializing. Shared generational experiences are one way, but certainly not the only way, of building these types of bonds. If you are the youngest in your institution, make an extra effort to connect with colleagues on other grounds, especially if you enter an already close-knit workplace.

Balancing all these perceptions and responsibilities can make a first job quite challenging—but can also keep it interesting! In the long run, your useful contributions to your library and your professional behavior will allow you to move fully into the culture and workflow of your institution.

Endnotes

1. Michael Watkins, *The First 90 Days: Critical Success Strategies for New Leaders at All Levels,* Boston: Harvard Business School, 2003: 1.
2. Roy Tennant, "Strategies for Keeping Current," *Library Journal*, Sept. 15 2003: 28.
3. Jill Emery, "It Just Doesn't Matter: What You Didn't Learn in Library School," in Priscilla Shontz, ed., *The Librarian's Career Guidebook*, Lanham, MD: Scarecrow, 2004: 255–256.
4. Geoffrey Bellman, *Getting Things Done When You Are Not In Charge: How to Succeed From a Support Position,* San Francisco: Berrett-Koehler, 1992: 51.

Moving Forward

As a Gen Mix manager, then, your challenge is to balance your enthusiasm for new young workers with genuine respect for the contributions of your Boomer staff.

Bruce Tulgan and Carolyn A. Martin[1]

Moving forward in your library career can mean any combination of moving up, moving on, or moving out. Taking some time at the outset to plan your career path can help you reach your goals and settle into your own niche more quickly. Of course, we always need to leave mental room for unexpected shifts, but too many of us drift from job to job without thinking about where we eventually want to take our careers. Next generation librarians are lucky to have the time to plan! Lay out your priorities and ambitions; determine the path you need to take to meet your own definition of success.

Whether you move on to management, decide to try out another type of librarianship, or just take on a new position with different duties and challenges, your willingness to keep moving and keep taking on new responsibilities can help you maintain your professional enthusiasm. Know the warning signs of a stagnant career, and be willing to move on or to work to transform your current job when you start burning out, becoming bored, or losing interest. As mentioned in Chapter 4, many NextGen librarians feel that some of their long-term colleagues seem to have burned out on the profession (or at least on their particular jobs) and lost their capacity to deal with change; avoid letting this happen to you. As you grow and change and learn, positions that fail to grow along with you eventually fail to meet your professional needs; you do neither yourself nor your institution any favors when you stay in a position that fails to use you to your full potential. One over-40 survey respondent suggests to her younger colleagues: "Love what you are

81

doing, and find positions that will give you real satisfaction—never fall into the type of thinking that says 'it's just a job'... It's not."

Moving Forward as a NextGen Issue

Moving forward in a library career is an important issue to NextGens for a variety of reasons:

➤ Those with much older or long-term co-workers need strategies on dealing effectively with the generational mix in their workplaces; those who move into management need to develop the ability to manage those older than themselves.

➤ NextGens need to establish the habit now of continually working to build the skills they need to move up or on when necessary (or advantageous).

➤ As fairly recent grads, many NextGens have not yet taken the time to look far enough ahead or to plan out their career paths; finding and settling into that first job can be all-consuming at the outset, leaving little time to look at the larger picture.

➤ As a group, NextGens tend to be more mobile than their older co-workers, due both to their age and concomitant differing responsibilities and approach to work. The willingness to be mobile and to take risks means that now is the time to move forward and think about where you want to go.

➤ Many NextGens tout their energy, enthusiasm, and capacity to work with technology and embrace change. They need also to look at the responsibilities that go along with becoming change agents in their organizations and/or profession.

➤ NextGens need to maintain an enthusiasm for the profession, and to be willing to think of moving on, up, or forward before getting to the point of burnout or career stagnation.

Some libraries are better than others at encouraging staff members to lead and at allowing them the flexibility to take on new projects and challenges. Some will not stand in your way if you are proactive enough to do so on your own; some will not have room for growth, requiring you to move on to another job or another institution entirely to forward your career. Your individual career goals and needs, as well as your institutional environment, help create an individual path.

Job Hopping or Career Building?

Generation X, especially, has been labeled as a job-hopping group with little employer loyalty. This stems, in part, from coming of age in an era of corporate downsizing and mass layoffs, watching as their parents and others were pushed aside by the institutions to which they had given years of loyalty. "Job hopping" may apply less, though, to those GenX and Y librarians who have made librarianship a deliberate career. How much job hopping stems from not knowing what you really want to do, trying out different paths before picking a profession? How much stems from a lack of employer loyalty, in terms of downsizing, lack of potential for growth, lack of flexibility, or reduced benefits? How much stems from the simple fact that some younger librarians are less tied down by family and geography than are many of their older peers?

This also speaks to the larger issue of younger librarians needing to be continually challenged and given opportunities to grow and contribute; perhaps NextGens are more willing to switch jobs simply because they expect more from their employers. It also speaks to library employers and administrators concerned about succession planning and the long-term future of their institutions; what do they need to do to keep, motivate, and train younger employees now? (For more on this, see Chapter 10.) One under-40 survey respondent explains: "I have jumped around a bit since starting in libraries in 2000. I'm on my fourth library job in less than five years. I don't feel like I have to make things work at a job that I don't fit well into. I don't feel like I owe my employers anything. I think that they have to make an effort to give me an interesting job with responsibility and growth, or I'm not going to stick around. My first professional job with my MLS degree lasted less than a year for these reasons."

Jan Kuebel, Library Associate, Riverside Public Library, CA, says: "Our generation intends to follow positions meeting our individual goals and character suits. We will cross library systems if positions appeal to our individuality. I doubt many of us will be satisfied with one specialty or library system for very long." Michelle Mach, Digital Projects Librarian, Colorado State University, Fort Collins, concurs: "I feel like I have more options—more mobility and possibilities of change. Sure, it's possible that I'll stay in the same comfy librarian job for the next 30 years, but I wouldn't bet on it!" Others are willing even to leave the profession if the right opportunity presents itself. Amelia Weber, Consultant, Lincoln Trails Library System, Champaign, IL, says: "I am looking for challenge and fulfillment, not just stability. I am willing to change jobs if that seems the right direction to take. I would like to pursue my chosen profession, but I am open to other possibilities."

Shifts in the job market also contribute to an increase in job hopping. Younger librarians may have begun alternative careers in failed dot-coms, being forced to move on as the economy shifted. They may have begun gaining library experience through contract positions or temporary work, an inherently unstable beginning. Fiona Mariner, Information Officer, Education.au Ltd., Adelaide, South Australia, explains: "Obviously the whole work environment is different—since I graduated, I've had three different library jobs, because most of what I've been offered so far has been casual/contract work. The whole "job for life" mindset just doesn't apply anymore." As the disparities between resource-rich and -poor libraries continue to grow, entry-level jobs at certain institutions also become seen as stepping stones to bigger and better things; hiring managers often realize this from the outset, and simply plan on rehiring every year or two.

If you do make a habit of changing jobs every year or two, realize that potential employers can view this as a sign that you will quickly move on from them as well; they may be less willing to make the investment involved in hiring and training you. Unfortunately, it is difficult to summarize your reasons for moving on in a resume—you need to be aware of the point where you may be seen as a bad risk. Those in tenure-track positions might be even more susceptible to accusations of job-hopping. If you decide to leave a tenure-track position without first achieving tenure, search committees might wonder why, and whether your decision stemmed from an inability to meet tenure-track expectations.

Different libraries have different perceptions; some hiring managers and search committees may wonder about those who stay "too long" in their positions, expressing concern about lack of ambition and complacency, while others may wonder about those who move around too often, expressing concern about lack of employer loyalty. As with any other aspect of the job hunt, your mileage will vary. In any case, be sure to leave any job gracefully, no matter how grateful you are to go. Give a reasonable amount of notice; usually expectations are spelled out in your contract or employee manual. The LIS world is small, and you will see these people again—or, they will see and talk to your future employers and colleagues.

The perception of job hopping can also affect intergenerational relations in library workplaces. Those who have remained in the same institution for 15, 20, or 25 years sometimes perceive their younger colleagues' urge to move on or to take on new challenges as disloyal. Some take rather personally NextGens' challenges to or dissatisfaction with a system that they as long-term staff have had a hand in creating. One under-40 survey respondent notes: "Veterans to the field still tend to harbor what a colleague of mine called a 'one-degree, one-career' mentality—especially when hiring people and considering their work histories suspect because of what appears to be job-hopping. Twenty-somethings may only stay with one job, performing well, for a year and move on to something else. Adjustments are going to have to be made! Organizational staffs are living, changing things, not established for 20 years and forgotten."

Employers obsessed with the question of employee loyalty, though, sometimes have justified insecurities about being worthy of that loyalty. It is easier to interpret a revolving-door position through a generational lens than to look at what steps an institution might take to improve its odds of retaining its younger and newer employees. Typically, these steps benefit all employees and help create a healthy and productive workplace; next generation librarians, for example, seek positions where they can have input into the direction of their libraries and work creatively with colleagues toward common goals. Employers and managers that pay more than lip service to participative management principles, and create an open environment that allows people the information, encouragement, and leeway they need to excel, will by default be more attractive to younger librarians.

Christina Seeger, MLS Candidate, Emporia State University, Portland, OR, says: "I am, as a GenXer, more likely to take a job that pays less but lets me have more creative input and work as part of a dynamic team. There is more value in the job, so less is needed in terms of monetary compensation. I am also more likely to change jobs in search of that feeling of accomplishment, whereas the Baby Boomers are generally more tied to money, stability, and loyalty to a company. That is an important concept to keep in mind while the library is undergoing this 'paradigm shift' to a more user-focused entity. It's important that the younger librarians are given the input into decisions that will not only empower them in their careers, but will empower the library to keep up with the change in focus and to compete in the changing environment of information." A willingness to move on also increases the chances that you will find the right fit for both you and an institution, and can reduce problems with burnout and boredom down the line.

The danger of job hopping lies in making it a lifelong habit—when you never find the right job fit, it is hard to see the profession as the right fit. If you are never happy in, or soon bored with, each position you accept, it is time to do some hard thinking about your real career goals and how to meet them. Never think of quitting at the first signs of friction; this is inevitable in any workplace, and you can often work through it.

Career Planning

One exciting part about entering the profession early is the luxury of having the time to plan out a career, part of which can include experimenting to find what libraries or types of positions best fit your needs and best meet your goals. When making your career plans, create both short- and long-term goals for yourself. Start by creating goals for your current position, then see how these relate to your long-term plans. Think of concrete steps to take toward each. Think of how best to move toward those long-term goals that less easily match up with those of your current job.

While employed in your first, second, or even third job, think about what you now need to do to eventually land that dream job. Will you need a second master's degree? A record of peer-reviewed publication? Experience managing projects and/or people? Specific technology knowledge or skills? Assess your current strengths and skills, and those that you are developing— or have the potential to develop—on your current job. As you did in your initial job hunt (see Chapter 3), take the time again to prioritize your desires for your next position. This time, you can afford to be pickier, especially if you are currently solidly employed. Think about factors like potential for advancement, geography, institutional size, work environment, salaries, and organizational goals and mission. Think about whether you want to move into management or work with a different type of patron population. Start looking at job ads to see what employers are looking for and what types of positions are prevalent in the geographical areas and types of libraries you are considering. Think about any logical series of steps you might take toward your career goal; see whether you need to work your way up by holding intermediate positions with increasing responsibility. (If your goal is to become a director of a larger institution, for example, you may wish to start looking at department-head level positions, or at director-level positions in small libraries, to gain some progressively responsible management experience on your way.)

GenX librarians with a few years in the profession sometimes in retrospect see the importance of taking time to plan and learn the ropes before moving up. Amanda Enyeart, Manager of Library Services, The Children's Hospital, Denver, CO, says: "Younger librarians think that they are being told that they should have to 'pay their dues' before being promoted to more responsible and powerful positions. I see it not as 'dues paying' but being patient and really learning the environment (political, fiscal, etc.), not drudgery for drudgery's sake. I was promoted fairly quickly into my management position, and would have had a hard time if it had happened any sooner. And I have learned so much in these past years as a manager, I can hardly believe that I was offered the position when I was." Over-40 survey respondents mention similar thoughts, as one says: "Everything cannot happen at once. Many younger people I went to class with were already looking for how to move up to bigger money. A few were achievers and we will see them in larger management positions, but most will burn out and get left behind. You need to establish your work style and library principles, including those you work with, before moving up."

Transitioning Up

Some academic institutions use a strictly delineated promotion process as well as (or instead of) tenure. Promotion here can mean a change in job title, duties, and/or salary. This can be both limiting and helpful for new librarians, who may chafe at specific requirements yet welcome clear guidelines. Keep a portfolio of your work, and document your accomplishments. In other environments, moving up inevitably means moving into management. In many libraries, taking on management responsibilities is also the best way to get the power to effect change—not to mention, to earn a decent salary. Even if you are not thinking of management at the outset of your career, remain open to the possibility.

Next generation librarians may move into management in a variety of ways. Some may decide that management is just not for them, and choose to build their own nontraditional career path, stay in a position they love, or try out a variety of different specialties. The graying of the profession, though, is purported to translate into a future glut of mid- and upper-level opportunities in libraries. The exact timing is up for debate, as are the exact numbers (see Chapter 1), but, at some point, many of today's next generation librarians will become managers and leaders. Think about the real reasons to move up, aside from the obvious salary considerations. Do you want more responsibility? Do you feel prepared to make decisions? Do you have ideas about where to take your institution, about programs to implement, about ways to motivate people or ease their way? As you move into management, you will gain more official power to effect change—use the skills you gained on previous projects to do so effectively. Get people of all levels, generations, and departments involved, and get involved yourself.

Whether you move elsewhere or move up within your own institution, a new position offers the opportunity to start fresh and to reenergize your library career. (Some will need to be reenergized sooner than others, depending on their work environments!) Younger library managers may worry more about the transition to management than older managers (even if they have the same level of library-related experience) because of concerns about managing people older than themselves, doubts that they will be seen as effective leaders, or fears that they will not be taken seriously. They may worry about others' perceptions that they are not qualified for the job. The best way to show that you are qualified for the job is to do it well. Realize also that management and supervisory skills develop over time; few managers, whatever their age or experience level, enter their first positions feeling fully prepared.

Some more experienced over-40 survey respondents had a plethora of useful and commonsense advice for their younger colleagues moving into management positions, including:

➤ "Treat all of your employees with respect and dignity, and try to get along with staff on every level from the maintenance person to the top person. Do not treat your employees like children and watch everything they do. Train all of your staff well, on procedures, etc., and be aware of training events that will benefit your staff. If at all possible, work with them on their scheduling, and don't be so rigid as to make your employees sorry they are working for you. Food helps once in a while."

➤ "Your budget will be cut. Your boss will not understand you. The library may be treated like the ugly stepsister. Learn to live with it. Learn to show your strengths. Show that the library is an essential part of every organization. Stand up for what you believe in."

➤ "Be kind to all! As a paraprofessional who is migrating into the professional realm, I am sickened by the hierarchy. The jobs performed by staff, students, and volunteers are just as important as the roles assigned to librarians. The work is different, not 'less-than.' "

➤ "Keep an open mind and an open heart. Listen to the feedback and comments of your employees. They may be closer to the problem than you are as a manager."

➤ "Do not stay behind closed doors. Move around, and listen. Take the circulation or reference desk from time to time, asking staff to show you what problems they are facing. How can you make informed decisions if you do not have a hands-on knowledge of what your staff experiences on a day-to-day basis? Your ability to manage will be equal to how much you understand the daily activities of your library."

➤ "Rather than thinking that you know it all, talk with those who are older (respected) and currently in management, discuss issues, and create solutions together."

➤ "Be flexible. Don't ignore personnel issues, even though it's tempting, given how many issues there are to address in any library these days. Your people, not your collections, are your best asset, so do what you can to keep them satisfied professionally. Communication is everything—even when the news is bad, it's better to be up-front about it. Your people will help you solve problems if you let them, but only if they know what's really going on. Management is a service occupation—to the people you manage as well as to the community your library serves. The balance can be tough, and you have to be ready for it before you decide to take on this role."

➤ "Be willing to make mistakes, and then freely admit them. Everyone hates the manager that keeps making seemingly stupid decisions but doesn't allow anyone to either be close enough to see why it was actually the right decision, or have the chance to guide them into a better choice."

➤ "Be passionate for libraries and library work. Don't let the 'been there, done that' mentality get you down.
Understand that there may be folks who resent being managed by a younger person. Understand the whole picture … every single person who works in your library is instrumental in keeping the library running well.
Understand that it's not quick, and it's not easy, but it is worth it."

Think about the advantages of moving up or taking on management responsibilities, even if the immediate monetary payoff is minimal. You have a lengthy library career ahead of you, and the more responsibility you take on now, the more opportunities will open up to you along the way. As a manager, you also have more official power to effect change, and to serve as an example of a next generation librarian doing well in a position of responsibility. NextGens have little call to complain about the ways their institutions are run, if they are unwilling to step up.

Many librarians, though, have little desire to manage, and you will have more choice among upper-level positions if you are ambitious in working your way up. On your way, be eager to lead projects, especially team-building and cross-departmental projects; this shows your ability to manage and increases your visibility and marketability. Those in hiring positions often look for a proven ability to lead; if you want to manage, take opportunities to build these skills and your portfolio along the way.

Unfortunately, some NextGens have a fairly negative view of library management. An August 2004 *American Libraries* letter, for example, responding to an earlier article on what future leaders and managers need to know, pointed out that Generation X librarians love the profession, but that " … there is no amount of money or prestige that would entice us to sacrifice our families, our home lives, and our sanity for the long hours and Sisyphean ordeal of a directorship … It's not that we are reluctant to assume leadership roles, it is just that no one has shown us a good enough reason why we should."[2] It is worth thinking about how much of this image is due to the actions of current supervisors and managers, and about how NextGens might do things differently. (Find more on balance in Chapter 8.)

Moving up within your own organization, while initially more comfortable than changing institutions, presents singular challenges. If your library fails to fill your old position quickly, you may end up doing both jobs for some time. If you are promoted over long-term or older co-workers, you may face a certain resentment. Realize, though, that you might have been promoted over long-term employees precisely because they lacked any desire—or ability—to move into management, or because they grew complacent in their careers and failed to be proactive or remain current. If you supervise pages, teen volunteers, work-study MLS students, interns, or others who may be closer to you in age and/or education level, you may have difficulty maintaining a professional relationship. Pay attention to these potential pitfalls and remain professional in all your interactions.

It can also be difficult for your former peers to adjust to having you as a manager. It is easy to form close friendships on the job, especially if you have moved to take a position and left behind your peer group in another town. Managers need to be managers first and friends second, and this is a huge realization for both you and your colleagues. As a manager, though, your one big plus is the ability to work for the benefit of your staff—you know the concerns you had as an entry-level librarian; now, how can you improve things for those who follow?

Supervising long-term, older employees presents its own issues. Some may have difficulty adjusting to being managed by someone the age of their own children. Younger librarians who move into management may find that their direct reports are all older and have more years of library experience. This makes for a difficult transition, as Anna Winkel, Branch Manager, Fraser Valley Library Branch of the Grand County Library District, Fraser, CO, notes: "I think that the most difficult thing about my age is managing people who are significantly older, because we have such different views of a workplace and how a 'boss' should behave. I try to make our library a fun place to work, with a collaborative decision-making team atmosphere. Some of the members of the staff here are very resistant to my style." Another under-40 survey respondent says: "Theoretically, supervising persons the same age as your parents is part of the job. In my first job, this was the most difficult thing to deal with. My respect for elders prevented me from being honest with my employees and correcting their mistakes and bad behavior. Likewise, those older workers failed to accept my authority over them. My leadership style is collaborative and I'm not one to throw around power and authority, but the total lack of respect that workers had for me was shocking." Avoid the mistake of not acting managerial because your priority is to be liked. Being too casual with some older employees, further, can be seen as a lack of respect.

Take the time to build mutual respect. You must demonstrate the same respect for your Boomer and Veteran staff as you want them to have for you. It is temptingly easy to make the mistake of letting your enthusiasm for younger staff members who may better match your own viewpoints over-shadow the very real contributions and accumulated institutional expertise of long-time staff. If you want to be taken seriously by your staff, you need to show them that you take them seriously in return. This is an integral part of any management relationship, regardless of the ages of the parties involved. People look for mutual respect and support from their supervisors, and age or other differences become less of an issue once you establish this foun-dation and patterns of healthy communication. People are any library's most important asset, and need to be treated that way. Sometimes, perceived age-related slights are simply overall bad management practices. Good man-agers are fair to all of their employees, and work to create an environment where all will thrive, regardless of their age or position on an organization chart. They never fall into the "do as I say, not as I do" trap; accountability cuts both ways.

Part of your managerial responsibility also involves a commitment to suc-cession planning. If you are one of only a few younger managers in your insti-tution—or are the only younger manager—how will you help your library develop a plan to replace those people who will be retiring? How will you bal-ance the idea of growing new leaders from within with that of bringing in new ideas from the outside? How will you encourage paraprofessionals to move up? How will you convince your administration of the importance of making strong hires in entry-level positions and of planning for the future of your insti-tution? As one younger survey respondent notes: "Younger librarians are entering a profession heavily dominated by management a full two genera-tions older than themselves. With the (predicted) impending librarian short-age, younger librarians will need to find ways to quickly adapt into management and professional careers that have been filled by librarians with vastly different training and experience than their own."

Transitioning Elsewhere

Moving elsewhere can mean moving up, moving laterally, or moving "backward," choosing to take on less responsibility in a new position at a new institution. If you find that your first job is not a good fit, you have more leeway in choosing a second—the old adage about it being easier to find a job when you have a job holds true. Be willing to move on, and be positive about the possibilities of a new position. As Priscilla Shontz writes: "If your institution does not value the fresh perspective you bring to the organization, you may need to look for your second job, where people will view you as someone with experience, rather than someone fresh out of school."[3]

Realize that transitions can be difficult; leaving even the most bureaucratic, unproductive, or unhealthy workplace environment means severing connections with co-workers, leaving familiar surroundings, and adjusting to a new group of colleagues, a new set of expectations, and a new environment. Further, adjusting to a second or third job carries with it some of the same transition pangs as moving into your first entry-level position, and you will go through the same period of mutual evaluation and probing. One of the under-40 librarians surveyed explains: "Younger librarians might find themselves going through a period of 'testing' when they move from one library job to another. (I did.) There are some libraries that put the 'new kid on the block' through their paces before they become an accepted member of the staff. And sometimes it's unpleasant. Be prepared, and know your stuff."

When you do move on, realize that now, with some experience behind you, you can stretch out and apply for a completely different set of jobs. Why get stuck in the entry-level mindset? Push yourself and have the confidence to believe in your actual qualifications; take stock of the skills and experiences you have built up on the job and in your professional activities; rework your resume and weight it more heavily toward your library experience. Apply to prestigious institutions, for management positions, for jobs requiring several years of experience—for those that seem just a little bit beyond your current skill set. You are looking now for a position where you can stay longer, where you can grow, and where you have the potential for advancement. If you decide to make a lateral move, be prepared to address perceptions that you are overqualified for entry-level positions or for those requiring little experience; explain why you are the right person for a particular job.

Resist the temptation to ever badmouth your previous workplace or old boss. The library world is a small one that talks constantly, and you will encounter people from your previous workplace again, or will encounter people who know them. The question of whether to tell your current employer you are looking for a new job is an open one, and depends entirely on your relationship with your current supervisor and co-workers. Either way, give a professional amount of notice, and help make the transition go as smoothly as possible. If your library somehow manages to find a replacement before you leave, take the time to help train him or her and explain your job duties and current projects. If not, leave your projects in good order, and leave notes on what your successor will need to know.

While entry-level jobs are currently tight, libraries report an increasing difficulty filling upper-level management and specialized positions. This is good news for NextGens who have already spent some time in the workforce, particularly for those who envision moving up into management. When you do make that move, though, expect to explain your desire and abilities to interviewers or committees. You will likely be asked about your management style, the way you will handle personnel issues, and your decision-making abilities. The more related experience you accumulate, the better able you will be to answer such questions.

Energizing Your Environment

If you cannot leave, or simply decide that now is not the time to move on, then you need to find ways to make your current job a good fit and to renew your professional enthusiasm. Ask for more responsibility; have specific ideas in mind. Managerial next generation librarians that tout their energy and enthusiasm for the profession have a special responsibility to extend that energy to their positions, infecting staff with their enthusiasm. Those in non-managerial positions, though, need to learn to take leadership roles nonetheless. Offer to spearhead a project, write a grant, or expand an existing service. Be proactive! Sometimes younger librarians let their age hold them back, feeling they have less to contribute than more-experienced colleagues, or unsure their ideas will get a fair reception. Sometimes they let their co-workers hold them back, not wanting to step on toes or encroach on others' turf. Sometimes they let their managers hold them back, feeling they need direction for their actions, rather than taking the initiative themselves.

Further, many NextGen librarians are used to being given external challenges, especially those who are recent grads or in their first job. Schools set out a list of required courses, or lay out a series of logical steps toward the degree. Professors assign research projects, homework, papers, and group tasks, often with very clear expectations. Managers, on the other hand, tend to throw new employees into a first full-time professional position, often with little or no training or orientation—giving you the task of making sense of those duties. Many NextGens are less used to creating their own internal motivations and outlining their own challenges.

Here is the truth: The more you prove your worth to your organization, the more leeway you will have in creating your own projects and charting your own path. One way to prove your worth? Spearhead a successful project! This is a healthy, self-perpetuating cycle. Take on challenges, offer solutions, and never be afraid to speak up. Again, though, go in understanding the situation and environmental variables—learn before reacting.

Anna Winkel explains: "I think we bring a flexible attitude that will continue to make using libraries easier. The younger librarians I work with are always looking for ways to make our patrons' experience better. We are unique in our enthusiasm and energy, which may wane as we get older, but will hopefully be supplemented by another generation of new librarians with new ideas." As mentioned in Chapter 3, one of the main complaints from surveyed next generation librarians was that their institutions and co-workers seemed overly resistant to needed changes, suffering from the "but we've always done it this way" syndrome. How can NextGens work to overcome workplace stagnation, and become change agents in their libraries? If you lack the control to change your workplace environment or your specific job, your only two options are to live with and adapt to it, or to leave it and move on (see previous sections).

Lifelong Learning

It may seem odd to talk about lifelong learning when you are likely at the outset of your library career, but, as with so many other things, starting out as you mean to continue can make all the difference. Library school and/or your first library job are just the beginning of your lifelong learning about librarianship. Those who establish the habit of continually learning and growing from the beginning will reap happy side effects, including a reduced chance of burnout, the ability to stave off boredom, and the opportunity to maximize employability. A constantly evolving profession creates the need to keep changing, growing, and learning as well—recent graduation or not. One under-40 respondent puts it succinctly, saying that "once a young librarian leaves library school, he or she should make sure to stay current. Our times are dynamic and fluent, so we have to be dynamic and fluent as well."

Roy Tennant reinforces this point, saying: "Learn all the time without even thinking about it. We are born to learn, but somewhere along the way many of us pick up the idea that we must be taught in order to learn. We think that if someone doesn't stand up in front of us and talk to us with either a chalkboard or PowerPoint slides, we cannot learn. We must regain our sense of wonder and our desire to learn."[4] NextGen librarians must *retain* their sense of wonder and desire to learn!

Online Continuing Education Resources

Why online? These resources are often low-cost or even free, so the smallest library or poorest individual can afford to take advantage of them, with the added plus of no travel required. Some representative ideas are listed here; many library systems and organizations are now getting on board and offering their own online continuing education to members.

➤ ALA's Continuing Education Clearinghouse, www.ala.org/ce/
   A searchable database of continuing education opportunities offered by ALA and its units. Includes both on-ground workshops and online learning.

➤ BCR, www.bcr.org/training/workshops/ web-based.html
   Both OCLC and non-OCLC workshops, including Web design, cataloging, and ILL.

➤ Beyond the Job, librarycareers.blogspot.com
   This Weblog links to professional development opportunities for librarians, from continuing education, to calls for proposals, to articles on career development topics.

➤ Dynix Institute, www.dynix.com/institute/
   Vendors such as SirsiDynix "give back" to the library community by providing a free series of online seminars given by leading professionals. Topics have ranged from conflict management to community outreach to open source software; older seminars are archived and freely available.

➤ InfoPeople, www.infopeople.org/training/
   The California-based InfoPeople offers online workshops on topics from reference fundamentals to "extreme Googling." Cost is subsidized for California residents, but quite a bit pricier for out-of-state attendees.

➤ PALINET, www.palinet.org/services/edprogram/ catalog/onlinecalendar.asp?Type=online
   Online workshops in a number of different areas, from OCLC ILL to Dreamweaver basics.

➤ SLA, www.sla.org/content/learn/learnmore/index.cfm
   Offers online seminars on topics from career development to creating Weblogs; some, though, can be somewhat pricey.

➤ WebJunction, www.webjunction.org
   WebJunction offers both free and low-cost online courses on topics from managing public-access computing to fundraising. Choose "Learning Center" and then an area of interest to see what is available.

   Individual library schools often offer online continuing education coursework; see the University of Maryland's College of Information Studies at www.clis. umd.edu/ce/index.html for an example. Associations such as ARL give online classes as well (see the ALA Clearinghouse, mentioned in this sidebar), but these are often cost-prohibitive for individuals and smaller institutions.

Take advantage of any professional development opportunities your institution affords; bring ideas to your supervisor's or administration's attention. Some universities' HR departments offer ongoing workshops or training opportunities to all employees; these can be useful to academic librarians. Many library systems offer free or subsidized workshops to all members, either in-person or online. Your alma mater may offer reduced-price classes to alumni, or even post-graduate certification programs, and your alumni association may invite speakers or sponsor workshops. Your local community college likely offers low-cost classes on Web design and other transferable skills. Think broadly.

This fits in with the earlier discussion of planning your career path—target the skills you need to develop or things you need to know, then find out where you can get those skills or learn those things. Identify opportunities through your professional reading and lists, or by following professional development Weblogs such as Beyond the Job (see sidebar on page 96). Look also at the section entitled "Keeping Up" in Chapter 7.

Ideas for more formal learning include earning certifications, stacking up continuing education credits, going back for a PhD, or working toward a second master's. A second subject master's, or even a subject PhD, can be especially helpful in an academic environment. This need is, of course, controversial, when the MLS is supposed to be the terminal degree, but an additional degree nonetheless can be an advantage in many environments. Think about what you need for your long-term career goals. Will an MPA or MBA be useful? Will your library provide funding for any of your coursework, or do you qualify for free or reduced tuition as a university employee? Taking courses outside the library field sometimes lets us reenergize ourselves and bring in nonlibrary skills that can be useful in expanding our horizons.

As librarians, everything we ever learn—no matter the venue—at some point comes in handy. Keep this in mind, and work to maximize the opportunities for your own learning from the outset of your career. Always think about the next step, and about where your career, your institution, and your profession are headed; keep yourself prepared for what may come. Learning and keeping involved helps our minds stay flexible and ready for the next thing—no matter what that may be.

Endnotes

1. Bruce Tulgan and Carolyn A. Martin, *Managing the Generation Mix: From Collision to Collaboration,* Amherst: HRD Press, 2002: 26.
2. Anna Marie Johnson, letter to the editor, *American Libraries* August 2004: 36.
3. Priscilla Shontz, *Jump Start Your Career In Library and Information Science,* New York: Scarecrow, 2002: 66.
4. Roy Tennant, "Strategies for Keeping Current," *Library Journal*, Sept. 15, 2003: 28.

6

Image, Stereotypes, and Diversity

... there seems to be no profession as preoccupied with self-examination as that of librarianship. While some of it may stem from an identity crisis, the refrain heard over and over is startlingly similar to Dangerfield's 'I don't get no respect.'
Wendi Arant and Candace R. Benefiel[1]

From shushing action figures to Marian the Librarian, next generation librarians have joined a profession with some powerful imagery attached. Whether encountered in person ("But you aren't quiet enough to be a librarian!"), in the media ("Librarian by day ... Bacardi by night"), or from patrons ("It must be nice to be able to read books all day"), focusing too closely on existing images can be both frustrating and tiring. Our obsession with our image has even led to Web sites such as the Fashionista Librarian (www.geocities.com/fashionistalibrarian/), whose author writes an associated blog and compiles suggestions of where to buy affordable yet fashionable work clothing. Some of us seem inclined to put as much emphasis on image as we do on our professional challenges.

Though it may seem we have talked "the image thing" to death, image and next generation librarianship are closely linked in many people's minds. And there's no denying that the way librarians are viewed affects both the profession's connections with the larger community and the ways in which libraries and library workers are—or are not—valued by society. Thus, it is worthwhile to take another look at these connections and perceptions from the NextGen perspective.

Sometimes our image hurts the profession—when politicians cut funding because they don't expect opposition from the meek library set; when people are discouraged from considering a profession where no one looks like

99

them; or when people are driven away by images of dull or forbidding libraries and librarians. One under-40 survey respondent says: "But really, I think a lot of the image stuff is superficial. The real change needs to come, not in the image of librarians, but in their value and place within society. The problem is not the image, but the fact that the librarian is always the first position to be cut in times of budget hurt. We need to worry less about the 'image' and more about the value of librarians." Another explains: "The stereotypical image hurts all librarians to the extent people think we are no longer applicable to today's information world, where I think we are more needed than ever."

Beyond impacting the public's image of librarians in general, NextGens who come from a variety of backgrounds are entering and impacting the profession, at a time when it is actively trying to recruit diverse members and serve diverse populations of users. Diversity issues of course go much deeper than our surface image, but in themselves help challenge people's stereotypes of librarians and librarianship. Generation X and Y, as the most diverse American generations, should help transform the makeup of the profession. Pixey Anne Mosley writes: "One positive effect of infusing the profession with Generation X, Generation Y, and Generation D [digital] may be to introduce more tolerance and acceptance of diversity initiatives to enable the profession to better reflect the population ethnicity demographics in the U.S. According to Raines, the Generation Xers are considerably more comfortable with diversity issues than previous generations."[2]

Image, Stereotypes, and Diversity as NextGen Issues

Our image as librarians, the stereotypes our patrons hold about us (and that we hold about each other), and our increasingly diverse population and profession are both general and particularly NextGen issues:

> ➤ Especially on the younger side, NextGen librarians are used to a variety of forms of self-expression, some of which can be at odds with conservative workplace norms and patron expectations.

> ➤ Younger librarians are subject to a number of generation-specific stereotypes from their colleagues,

patrons, and supervisors, in addition to the general public stereotypes about all librarians.

➤ NextGen librarians are also subject to forming their own stereotypes of co-workers and about the profession, and need to overcome these in order to work together effectively.

➤ Many NextGens feel that a traditional image, in one way or another, hampers the profession during this time of change and budgetary uncertainties.

➤ Younger generations tend to be more culturally and ethnically diverse and many have grown up interacting in a diverse environment, giving them different expectations and approaches than some members of previous generations.

➤ The profession is actively trying to recruit new, young, and diverse professionals; these efforts over time will have an impact on the makeup of the profession.

Societal changes and the evolution of youth culture translate into a plethora of ways of self-expression, some of which clash with the expectations of more conservative workplaces. One challenge for NextGens who like to push boundaries is how to combine the need for self-expression with a respect for both co-workers and patrons.

Stereotypes Live

Librarians of all ages and backgrounds are subject to similar stereotypes about the profession. Some under-40 survey respondents were surprised about the extent to which stereotypes still abound, offended by people's images of librarians and the profession, and emphatic in their efforts to challenge these, saying:

➤ "I was most surprised by the reactions of others to my profession. Questions like 'Where's your hairbun?' and 'You need a master's degree to shush people?' have quelled my initial enthusiasm to tell others what I do. I guess I didn't realize how widespread the stereotypes of librarians are. Not everyone realizes how amazingly interesting my job is."

➤ "I *hate* the stereotypical librarian image! I am totally offended by it. It has a negative effect on my relationship in the profession, but it also drives me to succeed in areas and ways that I feel are beneficial to the profession and will change such images. This includes becoming more knowledgeable and involved with info technology-related areas and supporting association-related products that I feel reflect on the profession more positively (e.g., the NJ Library Association Super Librarian campaign and anything with the words 'radical' or 'NextGen' librarian)."

➤ "Well, it occasionally makes me incensed! I have written articles and letters to editors on the matter. I also talk about this issue with many nonlibrarians."

➤ "Try to make people understand that all librarians are not old ladies with buns shushing kids. I am young, active, and full of energy every day. I feel this is a stereotype I fight on a daily basis. I hear at least once a week: 'I have never had a librarian like you!' It is a stereotype I strive to break!"

Younger librarians' reactions to the image vary considerably, however. A number feel the issue is overblown, or that efforts to replace it go overboard. Their comments range from: "Oh, geez, just leave it be and let it die or live or whatever. So not important. Why do librarians continue to obsess over this? Who cares? Just be a good librarian …" to "Quite frankly, I like wearing my hair in a bun, sensible shoes, no makeup, wire-rims, and long, funky skirts. It's just me. I don't want to be forced into a 'lipstick librarian' role, which would be terribly uncomfortable for me." Nanette Donohue, Technical Services Manager, Champaign Public Library, IL, sums up a number of younger librarians' resistance to the purported NextGen image obsession by saying: "It's kind of hard for me to not be snarky about the whole NextGen librarian thing. For some people, it's all about fighting for your right to show up to work with Hello Kitty barrettes in your pink and blue hair and still be treated as an 'adult.' But when you get past all the petty, stupid junk, it's really very exciting."

Others take the stereotype in stride and even play with it, saying things like: "I love [the stereotype]. I celebrate Buns Across America Day every year. I think it's funny and cute, and a little sexy. If we let the idea of the shushing librarian piss us off, we're just going to be annoyed all the time. Have fun with it! Then look at all the belly-dancing librarians, lipstick librarians, Goth librarians, and *male* librarians out there, and realize that we can be ourselves regardless of any stereotype. Most people think construction workers are stupid, but I know some who read Dostoyevsky and write poetry." Every profession has its own stereotypes, and librarians could really do worse. As another NextGen explains: "I think librarians waste way too much time worrying about their image, or getting either thrilled or ticked off at any media portrayal of librarians. It's not like we're the only profession with a stereotype. There's the computer scientist 'nerd' stereotype, the lawyer 'jerk' stereotype, etc. I'm sure they don't devote as much time to image in their literature as we do. I can hardly fault others for imagining librarians as middle-aged and female, when that's what we predominantly are."

When Perceptions Hurt

So we know librarianship is far from the only profession to have its stereotypes. The main challenge is to understand where our popular image harms the profession. Is it hurting recruitment? Is it hurting funding? Perhaps more important than people's perceptions of librarians' physical image is the perception of libraries as dull, or of librarians as forbidding and foreboding. Most of us have an unfortunate tale or two of a "mean librarian" from our youth, and this perception does more harm than any ideas about shushing, repressed sexuality, or hair buns.

A number of under-40 survey respondents even talk about entering the profession *despite* these images from their own childhood, and as a result working hard to combat them: "I remember my library as a child was not comfortable, and you felt like you were a heretic if you spoke above a whisper. I never liked asking any of those librarians questions. I want to be able to change that—to make a library someplace that people now would like to come to, for any reason they could find." Some over-40 respondents agree with NextGens' impulses here. Denise Sharp, Emporia State MLS Student, Portland, OR, says: "I am not a shusher, and I'm not all prim and proper. I don't go so far as to have multiple piercings or tattoos or wild-colored hair, but I support those who do. I think it's great when patrons can find someone like themselves in the library. I want young people growing up to see libraries and librarianship as cool!"

Ramirose Attebury Wendt, a student at University of South Carolina, Columbia, explains further: "I think the stereotypical librarian image should definitely be challenged, but the old lady with the bun who sits behind a desk and shushes people is not the only stereotype we have to worry about. These days I see a lot of burned-out, older reference librarians who act put out when people come up to the reference desk. That kind of stereotype is damaging to patrons who will never want to deal with a librarian again if that's how they think we all are. But then, I suppose there are grouchy younger librarians as well. I just try to act like a normal person with patrons or students. I don't want to seem all professional and stuffy." Another under-40 respondent notes: "I also think the image would have less bad connotations if we had better customer service in libraries; we could take a few lessons from retail. A woman in sensible shoes and a bun can be fun—if she's not being disagreeable with you and is treating you with respect."

As Jennifer Bobrovitz and Rosemary Griebel write: "The traditional stereotypical image attributed to librarians, and hence the library, contributes to the perception that both are irrelevant in the 21st century. If librarians collectively and individually fail to change this perception, libraries and the profession as we know it will cease to exist. Librarians have all the skills, tools, and knowledge required to ensure survival. We are either unwilling or unable to understand that the power to change the perception begins with us. A positive personal experience with a librarian is the single most powerful influence in shaping a positive image."[3]

Transforming the Stereotype

Next generation librarians challenge existing stereotypes just by their participation in the profession; the typical librarian stereotype skews older. Some NextGens challenge the image deliberately, for example, changing hair color each month as a talking point for their patrons and colleagues; others challenge it just by being themselves. Rebecca Rankin, Adult Services Librarian, Northlake Public Library District, IL, says: "I think I challenge the image just by who I am. I always have patrons or even people who know me say, 'you don't look like a librarian.' Why? Because I'm young? Because I don't have my hair in a bun? Because I don't wear glasses? Because I don't wear floral skirts? Because I have tattoos? Because I talk loud and laugh? What does a librarian look like?"

Younger librarians whose personal images run the gamut from traditional librarian to tattooed twenty-something take a variety of approaches to the image issue. The question, though, is how to go about effectively combating stereotypes while still remaining professional—and without simply replacing one stereotype with another. Jennifer Grothe Jenness, MLS student, University of North Texas, Denton, explains: "I could go for the GenX librarian stereotype; you know, dye my hair an unusual color, profess a devotion to indie films and music, and pierce something, but that would just be buying into a new stereotype. Besides, I like being blonde." Fiona Mariner, Information Officer, Education.au Ltd., Adelaide, South Australia, concurs: "But the whole 'young hip and funky' stereotype annoys me a bit. As a reaction to the pearls and twin-set image, it's a bit too much overkill, and I don't like being pigeonholed!"

Those who are uncomfortable with librarians' image need to give serious thought to what to replace it with. Librarians have created a variety of interesting niches, from modified librarians to lipstick librarians. Some NextGens enjoy talking about their pink hair, visible tattoos, and Doc Martens—but none of these is unique to librarians, NextGen or otherwise. One under-40 survey respondent views rebellion against the image as counterproductive, saying: "Actually, how people view librarians doesn't bother me as much as 'younger, hipper' librarians who act like they are the first generation of librarians who are at all worthy or 'cool,' for lack of a decent word ... I think we insult our own profession and buy into the stereotypical librarian image when we younger librarians act like we are the first and only nonstereotypical librarians fighting the good fight against a stupid image that others hold of our profession." Others point out that the variety among next generation librarians themselves precludes a single "NextGen" image in opposition to the traditional one: "Not all 'NextGen' librarians are alike. I certainly fit the profile of being young and new to the library world, but I am also religiously and morally conservative, averse to entering an administrative role, and a complete and total nerd. We're not all hip, young radicals!"

Some NextGens also encounter pressure to conform to a particular "librarian image" at their own workplaces. Workplace norms of course vary tremendously and depend on your particular job, your particular (or less than particular) boss, and the environment of your particular institution. Young Adult (YA) librarians, for example, may find that a nontraditional image makes them seem more approachable to teens and helps establish their library as a "cooler" place to be. In other institutions, librarians battle ever more specific dress codes, often seemingly aimed squarely at those whose fashion

mores may differ from those of their more conservative boards or administrations. (See, for example, the 2002 outcry at the Queens Borough Public
Library's dress code, which forbade, among other things, visible tattoos and
body piercings as well as sandals and blue denim.[4])

Also realize that people tend to make quick judgments on initial appearance. Whether this is right is beside the point—it happens. Embracing an
extreme image can feed into a different set of stereotypes about GenX and
GenY; when NextGens choose to match external generational assumptions,
it is somewhat disingenuous to be disturbed when people make additional
associated assumptions. Those whose images deviate from the library norm
need to decide whether it is more important to find a workplace where their
unusual image is embraced, or to compromise on image in return for other
benefits, such as an easier time earning the respect of some of their co-
workers, administrators, and/or patrons. Those in hiring positions need to
decide whether it is more important to hire for conformity or whether to welcome and invite a variety of individual styles.

Generational Assumptions

Patrons' perceptions of younger librarians as a group also affect
NextGens' workplace interactions and ability to provide service. As Leslie
Bussert, Reference & Instruction/Ethics & Humanities Librarian, University
of Washington, Bothell, notes: "I think sometimes my age is misleading to
users, as they think I look too young to a) be a librarian, b) know what I'm
doing/talking about, or c) be taken seriously." Jan Kuebel, Library
Associate, Riverside Public Library, CA, shares similar concerns: "Until I look
like I'm 40, I won't be recognized as anything more than the library page that
got her MLIS."

NextGen librarians report being told they are too young to be librarians,
asked what their majors are, or informed that patrons would rather wait for
"the real librarian" to appear. (Though some elementary school librarians
report the opposite, citing their students' perceptions that anyone over 25 is
positively ancient!) Some library patrons—and occasionally staff members—
seem comfortable commenting on NextGen librarians' youth and presumed
inexperience, while most would not presume similarly to comment on older
librarians' age.

Some survey respondents, though, choose to see this as a plus, saying
things like: "I think in some ways it helps me a lot that I am not stereotypical;
patrons feel more comfortable approaching me because I seem to be more

on their level, not separate and apart. I always try to challenge this image any way I can." Another explains: "I think the stereotype is most devastating in representing librarians as not being on the patrons' side. That's the part of it that I try the hardest to challenge, because I see how uncertain patrons are about approaching me."

Others accept that these mixed messages are unavoidable, understanding that their age brings some uncertainty about their capabilities yet also makes them seem more approachable by many. Katherine Vasilik, Library Associate, Paterson Free Public Library, NJ, says: "Because I am young, I am often viewed as an 'assistant' or as a volunteer. The public sometimes either assumes that I am not as intelligent or experienced as older employees, or assumes that I am an expert in computer technology. I find that I must work harder to prove that I am entirely capable of performing the duties of my job. However, I find that my age and my attitude make me more approachable to the general public." Another under-40 survey respondent explains: "I try to complement the positive part of the image in that I'm still the intelligent, curious person that the bunned/penciled librarian is (though I never shush anybody!), but I'm also a cool, approachable, young (though youth is fast passing me by), and hip person, who is eager to help you use the library's resources, teach your library literacy classes, and make sure the sources available to you (budget willing) are up-to-date and useful."

Our Assumptions About Each Other

The images library staff hold of each other are at least as important as patrons' perceptions. In today's multigenerational library workplace, generational stereotyping can stifle communication and prevent harmonious working relations. A number of younger survey respondents express concern that their older colleagues fail to view them as effective professionals, due merely to their age. One law library assistant mentions: "I think the biggest difference I've experienced is the attitude of others. Because I'm young (I'm 28, but people assume I'm closer to 22), other (older) library workers seem to assume that I won't be as good at my job. Co-workers seem surprised that someone so young could be qualified for the position, or do it well. They're always quite surprised when I prove them wrong."

Respondents to both surveys expressed a number of age-related assumptions about their colleagues. These are worthy of note because they affect the ways we interact with one another, both in the workplace and in the profession as a whole. Knowledge is power. NextGens who know how they are perceived by older colleagues can see how these perceptions affect their colleagues' relations with and reactions to younger librarians. Long-time librarians who understand younger librarians' assumptions about them will be better able to relate and react to these—or to combat them. Seeing older colleagues' reactions to NextGens' age-related assumptions, further, can help younger librarians see where these are flawed, or where they can be counterproductive.

When librarians approach these assumptions without defensiveness, thinking about where they may spring from and how to get to their root, we improve our ability to communicate and to get past these stereotypes so that we can work together toward common goals. As Claire Raines points out: "Using a generational lens makes it possible to see how you might be perceived by others when working through a relationship issue. Simply being willing to reflect on your own behavior and others' perceptions is a key ingredient to communicating appropriately and improving your relationship."[5]

Under-40 survey respondents expressed a number of age-related views about their older colleagues, saying:

> ➤ "I think there is a stereotype for a reason. You still see many librarians who fit that mold."

> ➤ "I think questioning how things are done is something I don't often find among my older peers—they seem more set in their ways and don't want to bother with shaking things up."

> ➤ "No more shhhing. I still know Baby Boomer librarians who want to shh."

> ➤ "The generation gap really can cause many issues and difficulties that are hard to talk about. Many older librarians do not want things to change and resist it. They are sometimes unwilling to try something new or to trust a younger librarian."

> ➤ "Librarians who have been in their jobs for a while do not seem as open to new ideas and new people."

> ➤ "Many older librarians want to keep things 'status quo,' when society needs the library to continue to grow with it."

Some over-40 survey respondents expressed age-related viewpoints about their younger colleagues as well, including:

➤ "I see younger folks with their ideas set in stone; they are very inflexible, and this is not a good thing. I hear: 'This is what we learned in school,' and that is all well and good, but do not be afraid to try another way!"

➤ "I have noticed that they don't seem as interested in collection development or acquisitions. They don't know how to answer questions or find things without a computer."

➤ "NextGen librarians tend to be more narrowly focused. They seem to be much more interested in machines than in public service."

➤ "I see precious few that are attempting to build good leadership and management skills that will enable them to become future leaders. I have seen too many library organizations' committees and working groups being filled with more senior librarians, because the younger members are either too timid or too lazy to assume the mantle of responsibility and take the extra time needed to develop and hone good management skills."

➤ "I have seen some attitudes on the NMRT list that seem a little cocky/arrogant—but that is common with many 20-to-27-year olds."

Additional assumptions and stereotypes are addressed in topical sections throughout the book. It is worthwhile, though, to think about the ways in which you view and approach colleagues of different generations, and about how your assumptions color your interactions.

NextGens who stereotype all of their older colleagues as change-resistant and complacent close off communication from the outset. One respondent to the over-40 survey says: "I have heard quite a number of comments around [next generation librarianship] that reek of age prejudice and discrimination against older librarians, but this is consistently treated as acceptable … It seems that 'NextGen' librarians are supposed to see the age of their colleagues as a causative agent that is part of a larger picture of resistance to change, hierarchical power structures, institutional conservatism, etc. I disagree." Under-40 respondent Nanette Donohue notes that "… generational bias goes both ways, and I'm sick of hearing NextGen librarians bashing older librarians. Yes, there are veteran librarians who are very closed-minded when it comes to input from those new to the field. However, all veteran librarians are *not* like that, and generalizations hurt us all." Older professionals who see NextGen librarians as inflexible and focused on technology at the expense of good public service also contribute to communication gaps; we need to learn how we are perceived by others and how to find a middle ground. Holding these inherent views about groups of colleagues and forming generalizations based on experiences with specific individuals can hinder effective working relations.

As library workplaces become more age-diverse, these problems in perception may recede over time. Responsibility both to workplaces and the profession, though, requires attention to where NextGen enthusiasm crosses over the line into an unproductive "us vs. them" mentality, while NextGens' older colleagues also have the same responsibility when it comes to their own biases. NextGen survey respondent Carrie Eastman, Serials/Interlibrary Loan Assistant, Wheelock College Library, Boston, MA, asks: "How aware are NextGen librarians of the need to pay attention to and learn from our more experienced colleagues? Without their knowledge and work, we would not be where we are today. And they are the ones who have established the foundation upon which we stand and from where we grow. Are NextGens quick to dismiss the knowledge of older colleagues just because they aren't 'hip' to all the technology? Or are they tapped into the need to bridge the gap?" Expressing stereotypical viewpoints blocks off productive communication on generational issues—because any discussion in that area is seen as just more of the same.

Demographics and Diversity

Sheer demographics show that incorporating next generation librarians into the field, especially Millennials, should help create a more diverse profession; GenY is currently the most diverse American generation, with GenX not lagging far behind. The Families and Work Institute explains that: "As everyone knows from firsthand observation, the workforce has become more racially and ethnically diverse. The proportion of white, non-Hispanic employees varies significantly by generation. While 80 percent of Matures and 79 percent of Boomers are white, non-Hispanic, only 70 percent of

Gen-X and 68 percent of Gen-Y are."[6] Howe and Strauss also point out: "Demographically, [Millennials are] America's most racially and ethnically diverse, and least-Caucasian, generation. In 1999, non-whites and Latinos accounted for nearly 36 percent of the 18-or-under population, a share half-again higher than for the Boomer age brackets, and nearly *three times* higher than for today's seniors."[7] The exact percentages vary depending on the cutoff years used for generations, but the general consensus is that each generation is more diverse than the last.

In other ways, NextGens impact the diversity of the profession. Librarianship remains predominantly female, and some male librarians report that this feeds into people's stereotypes about them and their place in the field. As one under-40 survey respondent explains: "I get a few laughs or smirks from people sometimes when they find out I am trying to land a library position, as a male in what has traditionally been a more female profession." Another says that: "The public also very often expects a librarian to be a woman, and as a male librarian, I sometimes find it annoying that this carries over into some sort of internalized feminization of the field."

Others feel that they serve as examples, and that their generation of male librarians will blaze the way toward making librarianship more attractive to men in the future. Dylan Baker, Youth Services Library Assistant II, Ada Community Library, Boise, ID, says: "Personally, I believe I am challenging the stereotype by being a male librarian. I think that the next generation needs to see more male librarians, so boys and young men will understand that this is an entirely possible career for them." Mark Roma, Stack Manager, Greene County Public Library, Fairborn, OH, opines that increased male participation in a traditionally female-dominated profession should eventually help raise salaries for all, saying that: "... salaries are going to rise with the influx of male librarians and tech-oriented professionals who will demand more for their skills."

Diversity in Libraries

As Zemke, Raines, and Filpiczak write: "Today's American workforce is unique and singular. Never before has there been a workforce and workplace so diverse in so many ways. The mix of race, gender, ethnicity, and generation in today's workplace is stunning."[8] While generational differences can in themselves be seen as a diversity issue, NextGen librarians are also entering a profession with an increasing awareness of the importance of incorporating diverse people and perspectives in order to effectively serve its diverse user population.

Next generation librarians come into the workplace with an expectation of working with diverse populations and colleagues; that is just how most have grown up. Many find it frustrating, to say the least, when conservative boards and other powers-that-be resist seeing the changing reality of our institutions and the populations they serve. As one under-40 survey respondent puts it: "Any number of criteria could be used to characterize the experience of the 'next' as opposed to the previous generation, but among them would definitely be ... coming of age in an society with very different approaches to civil rights, ethnic and religious diversity, and the meanings of diversity, equality, and representation in the workplace." Younger librarians are also used to interacting online, where these types of differences can be less readily apparent.

Incorporating diverse members and viewpoints into the profession does more for librarians' image and relationships with their communities than anything else. Some next generation librarians are emphatic in explaining that their decision both to enter and to remain in the field was due in part to the desire to serve as role models to others, especially to those younger people who lack opportunity to see themselves reflected in their own librarians. When asked whether he had ever considered leaving the profession, one under-40 survey respondent said: "NO ... African-American males are too scarce in the library world now ... we are needed to represent and encourage others to join the profession of serving the public." Others commented on the differing types of questions they were asked on the reference desk and on patrons' perceived comfort level in querying different staff members.

Other NextGens take the initiative to join or to form groups that help them connect with other professionals and better serve their varying communities. Vanessa J. Morris, Adult/Teen Librarian, Free Library of Philadelphia, PA, shares: "I founded a professional networking organization in Philadelphia called 'The Gathering Of African Americans in Library Service' (G.O.A.L.S.). This organization connects library professionals and paraprofessionals who work, live, and/or participate in the Philadelphia African American community. We work together to ensure the equity of information access to the African American community in Philadelphia. G.O.A.L.S. advocates the professional development and support of library professionals so that they can provide the highest level of professional service with the awareness of the unique cultural information needs of African Americans." (See more on networking in the next chapter.)

Diversity Resources

This is just a representative selection of the available diversity resources in librarianship. Check with your own local associations and with specific schools for more.

Associations

➤ ALA's Gay, Lesbian, Bisexual, and Transgendered Roundtable, www.ala.org/ala/glbtrt/welcomeglbtround.htm

See also the GAY-LIBN e-mail discussion list at www-lib.usc.edu/~trimmer/gay-libn.html.

➤ ALA's Office for Diversity, www.ala.org/diversity/

Focuses on all aspects of diversity issues; publishes *Versed* five times a year online, with two paper printings at ALA Annual and Midwinter, and administers the Spectrum Initiative (see "Scholarships").

➤ American Indian Library Association, www.nativeculturelinks.com/aila.html

➤ Asian/Pacific American Librarians Association, www.apalaweb.org

➤ Black Caucus of the American Library Association (BCALA), www.bcala.org

➤ Chinese American Librarians Association (CALA), www.cala-web.org

➤ REFORMA (The National Association to Promote Library and Information Services to Latinos and the Spanish-Speaking), www.reforma.org

Scholarships

➤ ALA's Spectrum Scholarships, www.ala.org/spectrum/

Spectrum awards one-year, $5,000 scholarships plus more than $1,500 in professional development opportunities to members of underrepresented groups, including American Indian/Alaska Native, Asian, Black/African American, Hispanic/Latino and Native Hawaiian/Other Pacific Islander students. Applicants must attend an ALA-accredited graduate program or an ALA-recognized NCATE School Library Media program.

➤ ARL (Association of Research Libraries) Initiative to Recruit a Diverse Workforce, www.arl.org/diversity/initapp2005.pdf

Provides a stipend of up to $10,000 over two years, a mentoring relationship, and leadership institute to encourage members of underrepresented groups to pursue careers in academic libraries.

➤ Diversity Librarians' Network, Scholarships and Awards List, www.lib.utk.edu/residents/dln/scholarships.html

➤ Knowledge River (University of Arizona), http://knowledgeriver.arizona.edu

"Knowledge River is concerned with the special interests and needs of Native Americans and Hispanics as graduate students," and offers a full scholarship plus a $10,000 graduate assistantship or living stipend to about 15 students yearly.

See also the "Scholarship Resources" sidebar in Chapter 2 on page 26—most of these associations include scholarships specifically for minorities and underrepresented groups among their offerings. Also check with your state association and nearby library schools for similar local opportunities.

Internships, Residencies, and Research Support

➤ ALA Diversity Research Grant Program, www.ala.org/ala/diversity/divresearchgrants/ diversityresearch.htm

➤ Cornell University Fellows Program, www.library. cornell.edu/diversity

➤ University of Tennessee Minority Librarian Residency Program, www.lib.utk.edu/lss/lpp/minres.html

Further, ALA and other organizations are pushing to recruit a new generation of diverse librarians through initiatives such as the Spectrum Scholarship program (see sidebar on page 114). The closure of Clark-Atlanta's School of Library and Information Sciences, one of only two historically black colleges with library schools, though, might set efforts back for a while.

Overall, NextGens by their very presence help hasten professional change, both in the way librarians are viewed and in the makeup of our field. As over-40 survey respondent Janine Reid, Executive Director, Weld Library District, Greeley, CO, notes: "All generations represented in the profession strengthens it—it is just another aspect of diversity." Whether or not NextGens make an overt effort to battle librarians' image and people's perceptions about librarianship, deeper ongoing professional transformations are what really matter. As librarians and librarianship change over the years, so, too, will people's ideas about the profession.

Endnotes

1. Wendi Arant and Candace R. Benefiel, "Introduction," *The Image and Role of the Librarian,* eds. Wendi Arant and Candace R. Benefiel, Binghamton, NY: Haworth, 2002: 1.

2. Pixey Anne Mosley, "Shedding the Stereotype: Librarians in the 21st Century," *The Reference Librarian* 78 (2002): 174.

3. Jennifer Bobrovitz and Rosemary Griebel, "Still Mousy After All These Years: The Image of the Librarian in the 21st Century," *Feliciter* 47:5 (2001): 263.

4. See, for example, Michael Rogers and Susan DiMattia, "Union Protests Queens Dress Code," *Library Journal,* September 1, 2002 <www.libraryjournal.com/article/CA239506> 9 February 2005, and Julia Cosgrove, "Librarians Told to Dress by the Book," *New York Daily News,* August 2, 2002 <http://nydaily news.com/front/story/7899p-7262c.html> 9 February 2005.

5. Claire Raines, *Connecting Generations: The Sourcebook for a New Workplace,* Berkeley: Crisp, 2003: 168.

6. Families and Work Institute, "Generation & Gender In the Workplace," *American Business Collaboration*, October 2004 <http://familiesandwork.org/eproducts/genandgender.pdf> 17 March 2005: 32.

7. Neil Howe and William Strauss, *Millennials Rising: The Next Great Generation,* New York: Vintage, 2000: 15.

8. Ron Zemke, Claire Raines, and Bob Filipczak, *Generations at Work: Managing the Clash of Veterans, Boomers, Xers, and Nexters in Your Workplace,* New York: AMACOM, 2000: 1.

Connections

Building and maintaining networks across generations, organiza-
tions, and cultures is a way to learn continuously and to leverage
the insights of people who have a genuine interest in your growth
and success.

Warren G. Bennis and Robert J. Thomas[1]

Whether we do so deliberately or unconsciously, we are constantly developing connections with one another, establishing and nurturing networks of
co-workers, colleagues, mentors, and friends. When we talk to other librarians, collaborate with co-workers, participate on e-mail discussion lists,
attend conferences, join committees, share information, or e-mail librarian
authors or bloggers whose works we admire, we create connections and
form the beginnings of community. As librarians, we constantly connect and
cooperate with others; a collaborative spirit permeates the whole profession.
NextGen librarians develop these connections with various groups, including other NextGens, the profession as a whole, the surrounding culture,
mentors and mentees, older colleagues, and various groups of patrons.

As under-40 survey respondent Anthony Auston, Librarian, Homewood
Public Library, IL, says: "It's important to keep a network of colleagues and
to remain abreast of trends in the industry. While many of us may be somewhat introverted at first, librarians are awfully opinionated and can be quite
talkative. Once you break the ice at a conference, it'll be difficult to calm the
storm of conversations. Above all, I recommend participating in electronic
discussion lists. Most of us sit at computers for some period of each day;
this is a great way to stay connected. And don't stop reading!"

As you move forward in your career, your personal networks naturally
evolve to keep pace with your changing needs and with changes in what you
have to offer others. Mentors who helped you early on may transform into

117

colleagues with whom you can collaborate; the type of advice you count on may evolve from the initial how-tos to encouragement during your first supervisory position to how you handle tough management decisions. You may find yourself in a few years mentoring others, or even becoming the go-to person on issues you help to resolve now. Every once in a while, take stock of your networks; think about your various types of connections and support and about where you need to build these up, work to transform older relationships, or begin to take more time to help others.

While librarianship, in general, is a profession that thrives on collaboration, younger librarians have grown up in an environment where new technological tools and the flattening of workplace hierarchies have encouraged them to work together and cooperate from the start. Many are used to open communication online, where best friends are made in the course of chat sessions and ideas inherently are shared. These experiences affect the way NextGens as a group communicate and connect with others.

Connections as a NextGen Issue

Paying attention to making and fostering various types of connections is an issue for next generation librarians for several reasons:

> Younger librarians who are frustrated with their professional associations can overlook useful avenues for networking and making connections. NextGens also face the need to transform their associations and organizations to meet the needs of 21st-century librarians and libraries.

> NextGen librarians connect with popular culture and with patrons' cultures in unique ways, especially when it comes to connecting with teens or college students to whom they are closer in age.

> Younger librarians enter a profession where they need to build bonds with multiple workplace generations. As mentioned in Chapter 1, today's library workplace contains four generations, and we need to be able to respect each others' perspectives and to strive to work together and learn from one another. One over-40 survey respondent notes: "I attended the ALCTS program on

generational issues at the ALA Conference in Toronto. I
was struck by a comment from an older librarian that
younger librarians excluded her from social activities."

➤ New professionals have not had the same time to build
up long-term connections as their more experienced
colleagues, and, as newer librarians, are not always
encouraged or funded to attend conferences or other
in-person networking events. This creates the need to
deliberately build up and nurture connections in other
ways.

➤ Younger librarians who are able to find mentors, inside or
outside of their particular workplaces, are able to
progress more smoothly in their careers and otherwise
benefit from others' advice and support.

➤ NextGens often need to make an extra effort to keep
connected to younger professionals outside of their own
institution, especially as the only younger librarian in
some libraries.

➤ Building connections is a great way for ambitious
NextGens to gain advantages in their career and to feel
as if they are full-fledged professionals. Brian C. Gray,
Library Associate Sr., University of Akron Libraries, OH,
says: "I feel the easiest way for a newer librarian to gain
knowledge of the history of the profession, a connection
to the present, and the ability to lead into the future is
involvement outside of their job description. I have
decided to actively pursue actions within ALA and SLA.
By volunteering to work on committees, participating in
activities, etc., I have developed a strong relationship with
other librarians and the profession."

Making connections remains essential at all stages of your career,
whether during library school as you seek out and apply for internships and
awards, during the job hunt as colleagues put in a good word or pass along
opportunities, on the job as you seek input on establishing new programs
and services, or later as you begin to move up the career ladder.

Intergenerational Connections

Much has been made of the current "conflict between generations" in library workplaces. (See Chapter 6 for more on the stereotypes different generations tend to hold about one another and how these affect our work relationships.) How much of this conflict, though, is real, how much is created, and how much is the result of common interpersonal workplace conflicts that get interpreted through a generational lens? How much is avoidable if NextGens pay attention to differences, and consciously adapt their style or approach to better jibe with those of colleagues or supervisors?

Generational biases cut both ways, and are as useless when applied to all older librarians as they are when applied to all younger librarians; Next-Gens need to build connections with colleagues of all ages. Under-40 survey respondent Angelica Cortez, News Researcher, Fort Worth Star- Telegram, TX, says: "There seems to be a lot of animosity in the profession. It's young versus old. Special libraries versus public libraries. Big libraries versus small libraries. Catalogers versus reference librarians. We need to work together more and realize that librarians have similar responsibilities, and that we are all valuable and contribute much." How will NextGens connect with their multigenerational patrons if they fail first to connect with their multigenerational colleagues?

Recognize that more experienced colleagues, managers, or others can also serve as mentors and role models as you begin moving up the library career ladder, and can connect you with the network they have built up over the years. This can be a formal or informal partnership; some workplaces set up mentoring programs for all new employees, while some associations or subgroups offer mentoring programs to their members. If this is not provided in your institution, or if no one in your workplace seems a suitable mentor or a good fit, look outside your institution. Mentors can be professors or colleagues; they can be people you meet on lists, at conferences, or at local workshops and meetings. (See more on this in the last section of this chapter.)

Every generation of library workers needs to make the effort to form connections with older and/or younger peers. Again, a willingness to recognize where gaps in perception and communication affect our relationships with colleagues is the first step in bridging these gaps and working together effectively. As Lynne C. Lancaster points out: "In today's libraries, generation gaps can spring up just about anywhere, from work ethic to rewards and from technology to time off. The way these gaps are bridged will have a lasting impact on our libraries' ability to function smoothly and serve patrons professionally. The way these issues are managed will profoundly affect the profession's ability to recruit and retain four very different generations of librarians for years to come. Understanding what makes each generation tick can help librarians reach across the generational divide to create stronger bonds, increase professionalism, and, ultimately, serve patrons better."[2]

Cultural Connections

Asked about the unique qualities next generation librarians bring to the field, one under-40 survey respondent puts it this way: "Understanding of current marketing trends and popular culture ... GenX and Y's perpetual obsession with cultural minutiae and trivia make them wonderful candidates for librarianship." This connection with popular culture also works in tandem with efforts to transform librarians' image, as over-40 survey respondent Dana Tumpowsky, Public Relations Manager, The City Library/Salt Lake City Public Library System, UT, explains: "Clearly, next generation librarians are already challenging the image with their choice of dress, their understanding of the younger culture, and their mastery of media such as zines, comic books, Web sites, and Internet communication techniques."

Every American generation grows up more immersed in digital media than the one before, and NextGen librarians might well be the bridge allowing libraries to meet patrons' changing expectations in a gamer/TiVo culture. NextGen librarians looking at how their work and their institutions connect with popular culture will find a welcome haven in Sophie Brookover's blog, "Pop Goes the Library" (www.popgoesthelibrary.com), which she describes as "an ongoing exploration of the intersection of popular culture and libraries." Additional contributors have begun to add more depth to the blog, focusing on topics from anime and manga, to TV and music.

John Putzier writes that "... *the workplace is a microcosm of society*. The more aware you are of issues in modern society and culture, the more you can become a foreseer of workplace trends and challenges. It's absolutely fail-proof, and history proves it (emphasis in original)."[3] This is one way in which some NextGens' connections with popular culture can be an asset. Librarianship today cannot afford to remain separate from the world; our need to remain relevant demands that we abandon any notion of libraries as set apart from our larger society and the communities we serve. The cultural connections NextGens build and bring are one way of breaking down barriers.

Online Connections

Online interactions are now a natural part of most librarians' careers, but can be an especially important lifeline for NextGens who may be the only younger librarians in their institutions. These connections also are integral to those who are looking for mutual support and encouragement, or who need advice on their first jobs, their first job hunt, or their first management position. Libraries often allocate scarce professional development and conference attendance resources in order of seniority. This makes it more difficult for NextGens to develop in-person bonds than for their colleagues with more longevity, who can more readily take advantage of in-person networking opportunities. Furthermore, comfort with online interaction is higher among those accustomed to using it daily during school, when IMing friends, and so on.

Online Venues for NextGen Librarians

➤ aliaNEWGRAD, http://lists.alia.org.au/mailman/
listinfo/aliaNEWGRAD/
   This Australian discussion list provides "a forum for
   students, new graduates and members of ALIA's
   New Graduates Group."

➤ IFLA's NPDG-L (New Professionals Discussion Group
   Mailing List), http://infoserv.inist.fr/wwsympa.fcgi/
   info/npdg-l
   An international list focusing specifically on
   professional development issues and opportunities
   for early-career librarians.

➤ Nexgenlib-l, http://lists.topica.com/lists/nexgenlib-l
   "NexGen Librarian is a forum for library and
   information professionals, paraprofessionals, and
   students in Generations X and Y to discuss the
   future of the profession, issues related to being a
   young librarian, and to bring fresh perspective to all
   things library related. All those who embrace our
   entrance into the profession are also welcome!" The
   associated NexGen librarian Web site and blog,

maintained by Christine Borne, can be found at
www.nexgenlibrarian.net.

➤ NEWLIB-L, www.lahacal.org/newlib/
The NEWLIB-L e-mail list, maintained by Susan
Scheiberg, is mainly aimed at new librarians and
focuses on issues, trends, and concerns affecting
those in the early stages of their library careers.

➤ NMRT-L, www.ala.org/ala/nmrt/nmrt
mailinglists.htm
The official discussion list for ALA's New Members
Round Table, NMRT-L is generally low-traffic, but
sometimes contains topical moderated discussions
or interviews with library leaders.

➤ The Young Librarian (TYL), www.younglibrarian.net
Created by Katie Dunneback (see interview in
Chapter 9), this is a resource for young and/or new
librarians. TYL solicits articles in four main areas:
career, image, life/social, and technology.

NextGen librarians can use the online environment to connect with their
peers nationally and worldwide, even if there are few or no younger professionals in their own workplace. (See the sidebar on page 122 for some
ideas.) Be careful, though, to also remain connected to the larger library
community. While lists for newer and younger librarians offer a tremendous
opportunity for connection and camaraderie, limiting yourself to these venues can also limit your exposure to the rest of the profession, narrowing your
viewpoint. NextGens are as susceptible as any other group to confirmation
bias and to going through online activities with blinders on; for every NextGen
or new librarian list you subscribe to, think of adding two on other general or
subject-specific topics. As under-40 survey respondent Peter Bromberg,
Program Development Coordinator, South Jersey Regional Library
Cooperative, Gibbsboro, NJ, notes: "I think the biggest value of having a
NextGen community is that there is a support group for many entering our
profession. However, I think there is a downside to NextGens segregating

themselves from the rest of the library community and using the support group as a place to reinforce complaints. Part of the dynamic of creating an 'us' (i.e., we're 'NextGens') is that it also creates a 'them' (i.e., stodgy old people who won't listen to us or pay us decently). So, while I see the value in a NextGen community, I think the dark underbelly of it is the us-versus-them mentality that takes hold."

Online activity intertwines with every other part of librarians' careers. During the job hunt, online colleagues can forward pertinent ads, serve as references, mention job openings before they hit the open market, and talk you up to their own supervisors and administrators. Participation in various venues provides "Googleable" material for potential employers looking for evidence of professional activity. On this note, realize that your current and/or future employers are likely to be active online as well, so be aware where your words appear and how you are coming across. The support and community you can find online, though, are the main draw.

As WebJunction's Chrystie Hill writes: "In some ways, these [online] communities are taking us back to the roots of librarianship: a civic responsibility to disseminate, globally and without discrimination, all forms of human knowledge. The spirit of sharing more quickly and efficiently, across all kinds of boundaries, online, is reminding us that we can and should be doing better librarianship. All of this, and I don't even get to detail the absolute thrill of learning, publishing, and discussing within a culture of shared responsibility, ownership, and collaboration."[4]

Associations and Conferences

Association involvement and conference attendance can bring more than the obvious benefits for motivated librarians. Conferences, in particular, are a natural networking opportunity; at your first conference, you will find that the event is at least as much about the schmoozing and networking as about the programs and exhibits. Look into options such as "dine-arounds," which bring together those interested in a particular topic to share a meal at a local restaurant. Find ideas at newer collaborative efforts such as the unofficial wiki for ALA 2005 (http://meredith.wolfwater.com/wiki/), a collaborative Web site that allowed people to contribute tips for conference newbies; restaurant, hotel, and attraction recommendations; and links to events and blogs. Look at more official sources of support such as SLA's "Tips From an Experienced Conference-Goer" (www.sla.org/Content/Events/conference/ac2005/geninfo/tips.cfm).

NextGen librarians whose institutions fail to provide sufficient financial support for conferences can look into ways to attend on the cheap. Start by avoiding overpriced conference hotels (map out public transportation options from outlying, more affordable places; look at youth hostels and other alternatives). Solicit roommates on e-mail lists or from personal contacts. Apply for scholarships, which are available both for students and for recent graduates. (See the sidebar on page 26 for scholarship ideas.) Bring your own food—think about hotels that provide kitchenettes, or at least refrigerators in their rooms—and map out multiple vendor parties, meals, and socials. You may need to sit through a presentation on the vendor's products, but this is a small sacrifice to avoid paying conference food prices.

See what your institution will support, and think about what you are willing to do on your own to be an active association member. Some libraries will provide funding and/or release time only to attend state and local conferences, others have staff alternate years attending larger national events, and yet others have no formal policy because no one ever assumes there will be funding available and never thinks to ask. Still others give out one lump sum for professional development; staff can spend it as they wish, within prestated limits. Never be afraid to ask for funding, especially if you get involved in a committee, are asked to present, or otherwise have a "better reason" to attend a conference. Presenting allows you to get even more involved, providing resume fodder and additional networking opportunities.

Going to conference presentations lets you see what the current "hot" issues in librarianship are, which can help you on the job, in interviews, and when mapping out your career path or continuing education. This is especially useful if you are newer in the profession; the issues you covered in class may differ from the concerns of those currently in the field, and many presenters will provide some "how we done it good" practical advice that you can emulate in your institution. At local conferences, presenters are usually from local libraries. This lets you see what initiatives their libraries are engaging in, and you can use this information later during interviews or to spark ideas in your own institution. Plan out your time in advance to maximize your benefit; use the conference schedule online, and have alternate sessions in mind. (People are used to movement during sessions; if one fails to meet your needs, move on!) Popular sessions can fill up fast; try to arrive early.

While job hunting, think also about interviewing at conference placement centers—this gives you good practice, and helps you see what employers are looking for. Talk to people you meet at any event—you never know who might have or know of a pertinent position. Librarianship is a small profession, and, even in the electronic era, "face time" is important. People will remember you, and will talk to people who remember you. Visit the exhibits and talk to vendors, as well; they are chatty folks, and may know of openings or remember you if one comes up in conversation. Even if you are not yet employed, make up your own business cards to give out.

There is no fee to job seekers to register at the placement centers at ALA Annual and Midwinter—you are not even required to attend the conference, although it can be useful to do so. Placement centers are especially helpful if you are interested in larger public libraries, which are often looking to fill multiple openings. Even employers that do not have exhibit booths will browse the database, which can lead to interviews or invitations to apply for particular positions well after the conference has ended. Registered employers have access to your information as a registered job-seeker and can search for potential candidates; you as a registered job-seeker can search opportunities. Career guidance and resume review services are also available at many conferences. Dress comfortably (especially shoes) but professionally at any conference; you never know who you may run into.

Conference Scholarship Opportunities

Find some representative conference scholarship opportunities in the list that follows. These are often available for state and local conferences as well; check with your state library, association, and library schools to see what might be offered. Smaller divisions and chapters of larger associations also offer targeted conference attendance funds; check with those in your areas of interest or geographical location. Conference grants are often announced on e-mail lists and in association magazines. Never assume that you have no chance of qualifying; often committees receive fewer applications than they would like.

➤ AALL (American Association of Law Libraries) Grants Program, www.aallnet.org/committee/grants/grants.asp
  Financial support for attendance at the Annual Meeting or at workshops.

➤ ALA Grants and Fellowships, www.ala.org/Template.cfm?Section=grantfellowship
  Hidden among the various offerings are grants for attendance at ALA, PLA, and other national conferences.

➤ IFLA (International Federation of Library Associations and Institutions) Fellowships, Grants, and Awards, www.ifla.org/III/members/grants.htm
  Includes grants for IFLA conference attendance.

➤ NASIG (North American Serials Interest Group) Student Grant, www.nasig.org/awards/timedated/studentgrant.html
  A conference attendance grant that also includes a year's membership in NASIG; attendees are required to write a report, which will be excerpted in the association newsletter.

➤ MLA (Medical Library Association), www.mlanet.org/awards/grants/index.html
  Offers an annual meeting grant plus other opportunities.

Those who want their professional associations to reflect their concerns need to participate in them. You can run for office, join committees, vote, attend conferences, and speak up at membership meetings. Library-related professional organizations are desperate for new blood, and, whether they admit it or not, many are equally in need of new ideas. Some NextGens do see the need for associations to reach out to younger members in particular, as one respondent to the under-40 survey suggests: "Maybe there should be some sort of division in ALA for younger librarians where we would not feel so disconnected—a group where we could come together to share our concerns."

If you have to pay for your own association memberships and/or conference attendance, consider this an investment in your career. You never know what contacts you might make; you can take advantage of career centers; you can pick up ideas and tips that you can bring into a future interview or into your current position. Many associations offer new member, paraprofessional, student, and sliding scale rates based on income. Investigate your options before deciding membership is too expensive. Over-40 survey respondent Frances Roscello, Associate, School Library Media Program, New York State Education Department, Albany, emphasizes what she has learned about the importance of involvement: "Having been in this profession many years and having served in a variety of leadership positions, one issue that to me is evident is that librarians who stay involved with library professional organizations stay fresh and up-to-date no matter what their age. Those who labor alone become stagnated in their positions. I think since I am older and because of the professional positions I have held, I am seen as an obvious leader. However, age does not always mean wisdom; I would like to see 35–45 year olds in leadership positions. For that to occur they need to become professionally involved right out of library school, so they can gain the needed experience to lead."

Brian C. Gray

What role did professional involvement play in your hunt for your first post-MLS position?

I was told during the interview process and by colleagues I approached for advice during my recent job hunt, that professional involvement shows a great initiative. It also demonstrates a desire for constant improvement for an organization and personal development. The networking aspect provided by professional development is a critical component of finding employment, especially if you are interested in highly competitive positions. I learned that a few of my former working mates or colleagues had informal conversations at some point with people from the organizations I applied to.

What tips do you have for making the most of attending conferences?

Attending a conference, just to attend and participate in the "regular" activities, is probably not something most students or new librarians can justify financially. To get the full rewards that conference attendance provides, you must do a little extra:

1. Network with professionals within your areas of interest, because name and face recognition are important as a career develops. Librarianship is a small world professionally, thus everyone knows everyone else.

2. Talk to vendors within your areas of interest, because you will be surprised what vendors may have heard about potential positions. Vendors build strong relationships with their clients. You never know what might come up in a conversation between a vendor and an organization ..."I am hiring but cannot find the right person." Vendor: "Has ____ submitted an application? He just said he was interested in this area."

3. Many of the people you meet at conferences, you may never see again. Use the conference environment to build your self-esteem and practice your communication skills.

4. Knowledge of professional issues is important to most organizations. Stay on top of the current issues by attending seminars or special sessions at conferences.

What other advantages do you see for newer and younger librarians becoming professionally active?

By getting involved, a new professional can discover their niche and interests. Professional involvement gives new librarians a chance to develop the skills that will make them unique during a job search or in advancement within their current organizations.

In addition to associations and conferences, how else do you remain professionally involved?

I am always reading professional literature. I do not read everything and am selective, thanks to the many table of contents alerting services that exist. In addition to the traditional librarian sources, I read selections about computers, technology, business management, leadership, and resources from my various subject areas (engineering, mathematics, or statistics).

I am also active on various lists. By posting questions, starting discussions, or helping others with their needs, I am constantly developing my communication skills and keeping an eye on the pulse of the profession.

Is there anything else you'd like to share?

If you are a student or a new librarian, the resources exist to attend conferences or workshops on limited or no funds. Many organizations offer opportunities for students to volunteer in exchange for conference fees, or give away money for first-time attendees. Offer to write an article or give a presentation, in exchange for money from your library school, a local professional organization, or a friends of a library group. Also, look for opportunities to save a few pennies by sharing travel expenses, using a travel metasearch engine on the Internet to purchase travel or hotel rooms, or consider alternative housing (hostels, relatives, or bed & breakfasts).

Brian C. Gray, 29, is Engineering Librarian at Case Western Reserve University in Cleveland, OH.

Also look for groups specifically targeted at newer and/or younger librarians. Most welcome all newer librarians, recent graduates, or students, regardless of age. Examples of local groups include New York METRO's New Librarians Special Interest Group (http://metro.org/SIGs/newlibs.html), which sponsors meetings on topics like the (2005 Valentine-themed) "Heartbreak of New Librarianship," and Illinois' North Suburban Library System's "New Librarian Networking Group," for those with four or fewer years in the profession. Australia has been doing quite a bit in this area; see the ALIA New Generation Policy and Advisory Group and regional subgroups (www.alia.org.au/governance/committees/new.generation/), as well as its New Librarians' Symposia (http://conferences.alia.org.au/newlibrarian2004/).

ALA's NMRT (New Members Round Table), for librarians in the profession less than 10 years, is mirrored by a number of state NMRTs. These groups offer conference orientations, resume reviews, socials, programming, and other services to help introduce members to both the particular association and the profession as a whole. They often offer assistance to student chapters, as well as scholarships and other support for potential and new librarians.

More general groups and committees also carry benefits for ambitious NextGens. These groups offer one way to gain the experience and skills that you will not necessarily gain in your current workplace, helping you qualify for future upper-level positions. When you volunteer for committees, for example, the skills you learn can range from managing a budget, to managing a team, to creating a Web site. Roundtables and divisions of larger organizations provide a nicely defined way to get involved; some NextGens report that those targeted toward serving younger patrons, such as ALA's YALSA (Young Adult Library Services Association) or ALSC (Association for Library Services to Children), even make a special effort to recruit next generation librarians for committee work, because of their closeness to the issues. Many committees, especially NMRT committees, allow or encourage virtual participation, where members conduct most work via e-mail. NMRT even guarantees a committee appointment to any member who wants one—so go for it, and then do your part. Never let financial considerations deter you from becoming active in associations. Some committees require attendance at two yearly conferences, some at one, and some at none; this is easy enough to ascertain. Some committees offer internship opportunities; look at these as a way to get your foot in the door.

Beyond ALA, specialized associations such as SLA are sometimes more accessible and less overwhelming for newer librarians. Their conferences are smaller, making it easier to choose among programs and cover all of the exhibits. SLA has regional chapters that offer even more targeted programming, as well as subject-specific divisions. Also, look at subject-specific associations such as ASIS&T (American Society for Information Science and Technology) and MLA, which reflect the concerns of specialized information professionals.

Many NextGens choose to start their association involvement by joining local groups, which generally have cheaper dues and require less travel.

Especially if you are intending to stay in your current geographical area, start out by joining your state or local associations and making connections there. If you are not a joiner, you can still take advantage of conferences (at an increased rate), or investigate subject-specific meetings such as Computers in Libraries.

Keeping Up

A major factor in keeping connected with our profession is simply keeping up with our profession. (See also the lifelong learning section in Chapter 5.) As new and younger librarians, it may seem odd to already be thinking about keeping current, but the pace of change, the fascinating developments in libraries everywhere, and the variety of skills required in different environments make it imperative to make a conscious commitment to keep up from the very beginning. When you made the decision to become a librarian, you made the commitment to a career of lifelong learning.

Keeping up leads to the concomitant need to deal with information overload; there is so much interesting and relevant material, and so many voices contributing, that librarians need to learn to be selective. Try strategies like filtering e-mail lists into different folders, use an RSS aggregator, and do some triage to whittle down your daily reading, while casting a wide enough net to keep up-to-date. One NextGen survey respondent explains: "As far as keeping connected to the profession, I read a number of professional journals, but more importantly I read a number of blogs put out by librarians. As far as I know, I'm the only blog-reader in my building, and I get the news about what's going on before most."

Also, read your association magazines—and why not think about writing for them? Professional publication is an excellent way to demonstrate professional activity, and easy to list on your resume. Look at your professional activities as possible material for articles and presentations, even if you are not currently in a tenure-track position or otherwise required to publish. Writing for the profession provides name recognition and further networking opportunities.

Finding a Mentor, Being a Mentor

Those lucky enough to find caring mentors are more likely to move up, be satisfied in their careers, and get involved with the profession. Whether you find a mentor in your own institution, online, or through a professional association, just having a more-seasoned professional ear to bounce ideas off of and encourage you can be invaluable. Multiple mentors can serve different purposes in your life. Those in your institution can help clarify tenure requirements or unwritten expectations; those outside your library can help inspire you to publish or to apply for a job that seems just out of reach; those in similar positions but with more experience can help you deal with your Board or resolve political issues. Eventually, you will outgrow most mentor relationships, and will go through a period of transition where you need to adjust to each other as peers. Mentoring is a relationship, and healthy relationships grow and change to meet the needs of the people involved.

Over the course of your career, you will also find numerous opportunities to mentor others, whether formally or informally, on an ongoing basis or as needed. As we learn from others and nurture our professional connections, we also have the responsibility to "pay it forward." Connections run in all directions. Chrissie Anderson Peters, Librarian, Basler Library, Northeast State Community College, Blountville, TN, explains: "I am active in various regional, state, and national professional associations. I remain subscribed to several e-mail discussion lists to at least read about what others are doing and thinking about in the profession. I write articles when I feel that I have some experience to share and an opportunity presents itself to do so. I present programs at conferences. I read 'the literature' so I can communicate more effectively with others in the profession when I have the opportunities to do so. When someone asks me for my advice or opinions, I do my best to help out in some way (even if it's a phone call or an e-mail from a complete stranger who may have read something I wrote somewhere). I just try to keep an open mind and keep all means of communication flowing as smoothly as possible."

As mentioned in Chapter 1, a number of GenX librarians with a few professional years behind them have already found the opportunity to mentor their Millennial colleagues, and these opportunities will only increase as you grow as a professional. Remain open to helping out the "next next" generation of librarians and committed to keeping the profession moving forward. Several over-40 survey respondents emphasized both networking and mentoring as among the most important lessons they have learned during their own careers. As Barbara J. Arnold, Admissions and Placement Adviser, Sr., University of Wisconsin-Madison, School of Library and Information Studies, advises: "Continue your education throughout your lifetime. Stay flexible and nimble by reading widely and by being an active member of several professional organizations. Support your professional school through financial contributions, by recruiting other talented people to the profession, and by teaching and mentoring colleagues." Mentoring others also helps you stay flexible, energized, and young! The success of those you mentor becomes, in a way, your success, too.

Endnotes

1. Warren G. Bennis and Robert J. Thomas, *Geeks & Geezers: How Era, Values, and Defining Moments Shape Leaders,* Boston: HBS Press, 2002: 176.
2. Lynne C. Lancaster, "The Click and Clash of Generations," *Library Journal* Oct. 15, 2003, <www.libraryjournal.com/article/CA325060> 22 May, 2005.
3. John Putzier, *Weirdos in the Workplace: The New Normal...Thriving in the Age of the Individual,* Upper Saddle River, NJ: Prentice Hall, 2004: 4.
4. Chrystie Hill, "Everything I Need To Know I Learned Online," *Library Journal* Feb. 15, 2005 <www.libraryjournal.com/article/CA502019> 1 April 2005.

Work/Life Balance

The clash of generations is most important in this work ethic. While baby boomers will work until the job is done and have been trained that they should be thankful for their jobs (even if it means staying until 11 on their kid's birthday), new librarians are suspicious of staying after 5 p.m. They willingly give their employers eight solid hours a day, rather than ten hours loaded with resentment. They want flexible scheduling. They want to be paid for all the hours they work. The new librarians are trying to achieve a healthy balance between work and life—and work doesn't always win.

Ria Newhouse and April Spisak[1]

One defining attribute of many Generation X and Y librarians is their tendency to place a high importance on work/life balance from the very outset of their careers. Martin Garnar, Reference Librarian, Dayton Memorial Library, Regis University, Denver, CO, is typical in saying: "While work is important, it's not the driving force in my life." Traditional library workplaces—especially those that start employees out with two weeks vacation at most, have a habit of rigid scheduling, or have a workplace culture that encourages habitually working past scheduled hours—may not be accustomed to accommodating such balance. Further, those accustomed to managing budgetary fluctuations in part by increasing the workloads and responsibilities of current staff may find NextGens more resistant to this practice than previous generations. A change in outlook and priorities has also created an awareness of the importance of balance for everyone, as well as contributed to the erosion of the idea of working for one institution throughout an entire career.

Libraries, further, are often less able to compete with other institutions on purely monetary terms. Many librarians, particularly on the nonprofit side, pick this profession partly out of a desire to avoid the pressures and compromises involved in many corporate environments. Institutions and managers that build in a respect for all employees as individuals will be better able to attract and keep good people. Librarians' definitions of success are not purely monetary, but also include the intangible rewards of working in a service profession, of upholding the principles of librarianship, and the thrill of connecting people with information. Further, the fringe benefits in many libraries, ranging from comp time to vacation packages to tuition reimbursement, can be deal makers for many. Libraries that recognize this and stress that there are different types of rewards—and that live up to their own hype—will be most likely to retain their younger staff. Younger librarians who move into management and start effecting change in their own libraries can work when necessary to transform previous expectations and institutional cultures.

Janet Crum, Head, Library Systems & Cataloging, Oregon Health & Science University, Portland says:

> I also think that many NextGens (myself included) have a different view of work than previous generations have had. Many of us don't draw our identities from our careers, and view work as one of many important facets of life rather than the dominant one. In practice, I think NextGens will resist putting in lots of extra, unpaid hours to make up for cuts in staffing. Later, as more of us move into management, we'll resist the ridiculous work hours expected of some library managers and redefine expectations for the employees we supervise. I expect to see more telecommuting and flexible/alternative work schedules as we NextGens attempt to integrate work with the rest of our lives in more healthy ways than some of our predecessors have found.

This is, of course, just one of many ways in which NextGens can change often long-standing institutional practices, but it stands out as one of the more important ways in which they are likely to have an impact.

Balance is an issue for younger entrants in all professions, not just librarianship. As the Families and Work Institute points out: "Boomers are more likely to be work-centric than other generations. Gen-X and Gen-Y are more likely to be dual-centric or family-centric. (Those placing a higher priority on work than family are considered work-centric, those placing higher priority on family than work are considered family-centric, and those placing the same priority on their job and family are considered dual-centric.) Twenty-two percent of

Boomers are work-centric, compared with 12 to 13 percent of other generations. In contrast, 50 percent of Gen-Y and 52 percent of Gen-X are family-centric compared with 41 percent of Boomers."[2] Again, here, it behooves libraries to pay attention to shifts in their surrounding society.

Work/Life Balance as a NextGen Issue

Work/life balance is a major NextGen issue. This is made more pressing by the fact that some older, long-term librarians originally entered the profession because of its perceived stability; others have spent decades of their working lives in a single organization. NextGens tend as a group to be more willing than those in previous generations to be mobile, and to take the risk inherent in moving to a new environment. (For more on this topic for managers, see Chapter 10; for more on the idea of "job hopping," see Chapter 5.) Factors making balance a NextGen issue include:

➤ Changing expectations make the primacy of balance an explicitly stated concern. Younger librarians find balance hugely important; one survey respondent says she has already considered leaving the profession and that: "Long hours and lack of time for personal life are also factors. My job is important, but so is having a life." This requires libraries to compete to hire and retain the best next generation employees, and to pay attention to succession planning in an era where many younger hires are dissatisfied with their current workplaces.

➤ The perception among some older colleagues of the necessity of paying dues before even thinking about building balance.

➤ The need to make common cause with Boomer colleagues who are also struggling to balance the varied facets of their lives. Although the reasons may be different, the need is the same.

➤ The fact that NextGens are by definition at an age where many are starting families, making work-life balance a pressing issue for new parents, newlyweds, and those forming other bonds that take primacy over their work lives.

➤ The problems that occur when NextGens enter the profession full-force and fail to prioritize or target their efforts; the impulse to change everything at once and start multiple new projects simultaneously can easily lead to burnout or professional fatigue.

So, how do NextGens go about convincing their managers and administrations of the necessity of balance? Many libraries, even those who are "cutting edge" in terms of technology and related initiatives, can be much slower to move forward in terms of how they treat their employees. Their corporate culture and benefit structure have built up over a number of years, and any challenge to the status quo can be seen as a threat. Next generation librarians seeking balance often bear the burden of convincing their administrations of the necessity of change, and of the truth that flexibility and encouraging balance can improve both productivity and employee contentment.

Paying Your Dues

One difficulty in building a workplace that provides balance for all is the perception by some more seasoned librarians that the whole notion of work/life balance is merely an attempt to avoid "paying dues." This can easily degenerate into a discussion along the lines of: "I walked to work barefoot in the snow when I was your age. Uphill. Both ways ..." Any dialogue on balance, therefore, needs to be built partially on the understanding that opening the discussion can stir up resentment among those who lacked similar options when beginning their own careers. The expectation of balance can also seem very foreign to those who devote all their extra time to their own jobs and have the simple expectation that others will put in the same hours—especially when they manage NextGens with different priorities. The idea of personal fulfillment through work also is often viewed through a generational lens; younger librarians may be less likely to see their jobs as something they just need to put up with to pay the bills, support a family, or because work is just what one does.

Work/life balance is in no way a purely next generation issue, though, and needs to be presented as it truly is: an issue that affects all library employees. Your older colleagues may be responsible for caring for their aging parents, talking their children through crises at college, wanting to spend more time with their grandchildren, or simply reshifting their priorities, seeking to invest more of their time in personal passions they were unable to pursue in their youth. They may appreciate the availability of flextime, telecommuting, or other options, but may be less willing to make an issue of it at this point in their careers. Some may also remember when "we tried this before and it didn't work," a phrase with an uncanny ability to signal the death knell for change in libraries everywhere.

Balance at this point is also a retention issue; libraries today need to realize the true costs of losing and replacing staff members, and implement programs and policies that will help them keep their best and brightest. (Find more on retention in Chapter 10; more on the concept of paying dues in Chapter 5.)

Family Considerations

Family considerations for next generation librarians range from agreeing with one's partner on where to settle down to figuring out how best to balance building a career and caring for young children. Simple biology dictates that librarians in their 20s and 30s are those most likely to be starting families. Many at this time see flexibility as imperative. The relatively low pay in librarianship, particularly when compared to other professions that require the same level of education, as well as its continuing status as a female-dominated profession, means that librarians may be more likely to be moving in and out of the workforce than will their nonlibrarian partners. An openness to flexible options can allow libraries to retain good employees, while increasing NextGens' loyalty to their organizations and their managers.

As Tanzi Merritt, Associate Director of Library and Information Services, Gateway Community and Technical College, Edgewood, KY, puts it: "We expect to be taken seriously and not treated as if we are too young to yet know how to handle work situations, and we expect a certain amount of freedom and flexibility in our positions. We are no longer willing to let our work be our life, and we expect to be allowed to place family first. No longer do we see tons of people who are willing to work 50-hour weeks with no compensation." Valerie Nye, Public Library Consultant, New Mexico State Library, Santa Fe, says: "I think we see work life as a *part* of our lives—and not our entire lives. We are content working a nine-to-five day. And, for women, I think we feel we have an option when we have kids. It is okay to be professional and take years off to be with your children, or, you can stay in the workforce. There doesn't seem to be a social norm in this area for our generation."

Resources for Librarian Parents

Recently, some parent librarians have set up online forums to discuss issues particular to parenting and librarianship. The major two sites are:

➤ Librariansahm, http://groups.yahoo.com/group/librariansahm/
  Support for stay-at-home parent librarians, including tips on keeping professionally active and working from home.

➤ Libparenting, http://groups.yahoo.com/group/libparenting/
  A low-traffic group focusing on balancing work and family as well as family/maternity leave policy issues in libraries.

The question for NextGens seeking balance becomes how to get workplaces and administrations to meet their needs for flexibility. How will libraries learn that the benefits of keeping good librarians—and keeping them happy!—outweigh either the fear of change or the perception that those seeking flexibility lack commitment to their organizations?

Many librarian parents who have worked out flexible arrangements with their employers began laying the groundwork long before they began adding to their families. As a department head at my own public library, for example, I began telecommuting one day a week on a trial basis two years before my son was born. I originally sold the idea to my administration as a way for me to spend uninterrupted time on projects like grant writing, Web design, and collection development, which worked out well. (As the only "systems" person at my institution, I was interrupted with tech support and technical questions often enough that this made quite a bit of sense.) When my son was born and I went part-time, the telecommuting option was so firmly established that my continuing to do so while carrying out some of my part-time duties was never questioned.

This, of course, requires a bit of planning ahead. But those who can set up work-at-home or flextime options before their children arrive are able to establish a track record, showing that the system works, and that they are not suddenly seeking to back out of their work commitments. They also help blaze the trail for those who follow. If you are interested in working from home, talk to your systems department or the tech people in your larger institution about ways to resolve technical issues, such as setting up secure VPN (Virtual Private Network) computer access so that you can work remotely more effectively. You can also look into opportunities with organizations, such as Tutor.com, that hire virtual librarians. If you do have children, though, plan to do most of your work when they are sleeping or when you have other help; try not to get overly ambitious and then again find yourself balancing the needs of your job with the needs of your family.

Family considerations also come into play in individual decision making. When partnered NextGens settle down in a geographic location, they need first to select the criteria that will determine where they will end up. If you base your location on earning potential, following the partner with the higher-paying job, the librarian half will often lose out (unless you both happen to be librarians). If your partner is settled happily and lucratively in an area glutted with new grads, this affects your chances of finding entry-level employment. If you are both just starting out, will you move wherever one of you finds a job first? Near family? Whose family? Do you take turns? Does each partner have veto power over undesirable locations? Do you just take the plunge and move somewhere where you think both of you will stand a decent chance of finding satisfactory employment? If you are both unsettled, does the librarian in the family follow the other's career, on the assumption that there are one or more libraries—and therefore library jobs—anywhere? Are you open to working on a long-distance relationship if one finds a good position before the other, or to gain a year or two of experience in a less-popular geographical area before switching jobs and moving to join your partner? Thinking about these factors ahead of time can save some heartache, helping you avoid targeting that dream job across the country without first consulting your significant other or thinking about the impact on your family.

Librarian parents also face additional dilemmas. Many libraries are not large enough to fall under FMLA, so maternity-leave policies vary dramatically (although some leave is often covered through short-term disability).

NextGens in the process of starting families also run the risk of having to tell a brand-new employer about a pregnancy, or of finding out in the midst of applications and interviews and having to add a new factor into the job-decision equation. If you are in the middle of a tenure process, the tenure timeline may be a factor in your decision about when to have children or make other life-changing decisions. In institutions where you may be the first employee in years, if not decades, to give birth, you will need to be proactive in researching the benefits to which you are entitled. As a male librarian seeking paternity leave, you may be setting a new precedent. As a same-sex partner seeking paternal or maternal leave, you may be a trailblazer. Take the time to lay out your needs clearly, including a proposal for completing current projects before taking leave and what you plan for your return.

You may decide to take a break from full-time employment while your children are small—this is one way of achieving long-term balance. Think, though, about the potential long-term impact on your career, and about ways you will stay up-to-date in the interim. Much of the advice in Chapter 3 on staying professionally active while unemployed also applies here. If you choose to work part-time, again, it may be useful to figure out hours and duties in advance and to see how flexible your current employer might be. Try to achieve the best balance for yourself and your family; move in and out of the library workforce or full- and part-time employment as your needs dictate or as your dream job opens up. If you do choose to leave your position or to move to part-time hours, try not to feel guilty about leaving your institution in the lurch. Having a child is just one of many reasons you may move on, and should not be viewed as unique. No one—not even you!—is irreplaceable. While you should tie up as many loose ends as possible, you need in the end to do what is best for your family.

Many next generation librarians, of course, choose to remain child-free, or are child-free throughout a good portion of their careers. Both those with and without children, however, can benefit from flexible workplaces—as can their older colleagues. Whether you benefit from workplace flexibility for personal reasons (caring for an aging parent or loved one or recovering from an illness or trauma) or from the need to create balance by building in sufficient time for personal passions (volunteering or traveling or windsurfing), employees who achieve that balance are more productive, more dedicated to their organizations, and are more likely to develop the equilibrium needed to deal effectively with the budgetary and people issues inherent to working in libraries. Those who are single also have needs in balancing life and career—and some single librarians need to spend extra effort on creating balance, because they lack the built-in nonwork demands of a larger family unit.

Building Balance

New technologies contribute both toward helping build balance and toward allowing work to encroach on librarians' personal lives. An administration that allows telecommuting, for example, may also have the expectation that you will check e-mail or complete projects while on vacation or leave—simply because you can—blurring the boundaries between the facets of your life. Better technology at work can also lead to the temptation of spending a reference desk shift planning your next vacation online or downloading movies on your employer's T3 line. Blurring work/life boundaries contribute to the difficulty of achieving true balance.

NextGens can be particularly susceptible to burnout on the job because of their tendency to go in full-steam and tackle multiple projects and existing practices at once. New employees also tend to want to impress their managers and to prove themselves, leading them to take on too much at the outset. It takes time to learn the best way to prioritize, to learn where to challenge existing practices and fight the good fight, and to learn where your efforts might be better spent elsewhere. NextGens who get involved in associations or institutional committees, and who develop a reputation for reliability, will keep getting asked to do more: the reward for good work, of course, being more work. Learn to say no, learn to prioritize, and learn to get others involved.

Be aware that NextGens are as subject to burnout as their long-term colleagues. It does not necessarily take 30 years on the job. Entry-level librarians can be susceptible to different kinds of stress, because of their perceived lack of control within their organizations or a lack of encouragement to take on new challenges and projects. They can get caught up in the monotony of reference desk duties that seem to degenerate into nothing but signing up Internet users and unjamming printers, or they get frustrated by an apparent lack of opportunity for advancement in their current libraries. Try to recognize the need to move on or to take steps to otherwise reenergize your career.

Flexible work schedules are, of course, only one way of building balance into librarians' lives. Never make the mistake of getting so wrapped up in work that you forget there is an outside world. Balanced librarians are less susceptible to burnout, excessive stress, or disillusionment with the profession as a whole. The Families and Work Institute explains the importance of work and family balance and prioritization in its study of generation and gender in the workplace, saying: "It is important to note that employees who are dual-centric or family-centric exhibit significantly better mental health, greater satisfaction with their lives, and higher levels of job satisfaction than employees who are work-centric."[3] The same study also showed that many workers were uninterested in taking on jobs with more responsibility than their current positions. This is another strike for balance, but also another indication that those who do wish to move up will likely face few obstacles, as mentioned in Chapter 5.

Flexibility is only one factor in creating balance. As mentioned in the introduction, a whole confluence of factors come together to make us the people we are. You may be an expert scuba diver, Toastmaster, dog trainer, or movie buff—we all need to take time to pursue our outside passions. You are more than your job title. Further, librarianship is a career where anything we learn and anything we do comes in handy at some point. Michelle Budt-Caulk, Electronic Services Librarian, St. Charles Public Library, IL, explains: "GenXers also bring a balance to the profession. My boss, a Baby Boomer, will work like mad from 8:30 A.M. until 7:00 P.M., and take one week of vacation per year. I prefer to balance my work life with personal life, yet I am still involved in things that benefit my work life during the off-hours—as president of the local adult literacy organization's board, as a member of our women's business council, and as a consultant to WebFeat. As an avid traveler, I'm also taking every second of my four weeks of vacation!"

Next generation librarians can also seek out institutions where union or other agreements help to build in certain types of balance for employees. Many academic institutions, for example, offer their tenure-track librarians sabbatical or release time to pursue personal research, which can help you focus on professional but non-work-related responsibilities for a while and to create the peer-reviewed publications that will help you win tenure. This can be especially useful in building balance back into tenure-track positions that seem to require more than a full-time commitment, with service and publishing requirements on top of normal work duties. Other libraries do not mind if you use off-desk time to pursue your research or writing. Look at your union agreement; see what other librarians in your institution have been able to work out. A break from multitasking can refresh your commitment to the job and the profession, while also allowing you to complete complex projects that require extended periods of concentration.

Managers seeking balance need to move away from hierarchical structures and learn the power of delegation and empowering others. You cannot
be hands-on in every situation; letting others take on more responsibility benefits both you and your staff, giving them an opportunity to grow and develop
themselves as leaders. NextGens in management can also work to create
balance for their employees. If balance is important to you, find ways to
make it important to your institution as well. This is another way in which next
generation librarians can help transform their workplaces, and, by extension,
their profession.

Endnotes

1. Ria Newhouse and April Spisak, "Fixing the First Job," *Library Journal* August
   2004: 46.
2. Families and Work Institute, "Generation & Gender In the Workplace," American
   Business Collaboration, October 2004 <http://familiesandwork.org/eproducts/
   genandgender.pdf> 17 March 2005: 3.
3. Ibid., 11.

Transforming the Profession

The world of librarians is changing. If we do not realize this and change too, we, like the dinosaurs, will disappear ... Every profession has its time of evolution, a period of change in which the way it reaches its goals and fulfills its mission changes ... Our observation and response to this current period of evolution in our own profession is crucial to its well-being, success, and existence.

Anne A. Salter[1]

One exciting plus in entering the profession during this time of transition is the chance to get in on the ground floor of change, to take advantage of the opportunity—of the very *need*—to move the field forward. The critical mass of next generation librarians moving into library workplaces, combined with changing user expectations, changing technology, and a changing institutional image, translates into both the ability and the responsibility to drive change.

A number of NextGen survey respondents see it as part of their responsibility to work to change the profession. Jan Kuebel, Library Associate, Riverside Public Library, CA, says: "NextGen librarians are hungry for change. Libraries aren't progressing fast enough for us. Patience is not one of our better virtues, I'm afraid. We come from educational backgrounds that emphasize group work/teamwork. We want to see a horizontal organization chart supporting creative ideas, innovative strategies, and collaborative efforts with the promise of something bigger, better, and breathtakingly spectacular. And we have the energy to make it happen." Anthony Auston, Librarian, Homewood Public Library, IL, concurs: "I believe that we represent a vital kick in the ass of complacency. Our creativity, spunk, and motivation will help carry our services into the next era of information retrieval and help to redefine the essential roles of a community library." Some over-40

147

survey respondents see a similar mission for their younger peers; one says: "They are very analytical; they are smart, informed, and enjoy working hard on moving the profession forward. I think they will have to save the profession; are they strong enough to do that?"

Unfortunately, though, next generation librarians' approach to larger professional issues tends to be fragmented and divided. Part of the problem in articulating a vision of the future of the profession is that many younger librarians, who also tend to be new grads, are focused first on personal issues, such as getting a job and living on an entry-level salary. Others are dealing with an overwhelming fear of change among their colleagues, excessive bureaucracy in their workplaces, or the need to combat stereotypes about younger librarians in their own institutions. Before NextGens can put together a coherent approach to professional issues or a vision of our field's future, their basic needs have to be met. If I'm worrying about making rent and whether I'll have to take a job at Starbucks to pay the bills, then my concerns focus specifically on job shortages and salary issues—especially my own job shortage and salary issues—rather than on larger professional concerns. Those who spend any amount of time on a discussion group for next generation librarians or new grads will come away overwhelmed by these immediate concerns. Those who have settled happily into their careers can easily be drowned out; this is one disadvantage of relying solely on online communication, as the angriest voices are often the loudest and most persistent.

Some under-40 survey respondents express concern that their peers' preoccupation with generational issues can distract them from larger issues of true professional import. Michelle Swain, Director, Arkansas City Public Library, KS, explains: "I think generational issues are fun to talk about, and often intriguingly accurate, a lot like horoscopes. But I think they distract us from talking in depth about more significant issues: How do you get rid of people who should never be librarians in the first place, how do we keep our library schools open in the face of higher education funding crises, or how do we stop examining our own belly buttons and turn outward to our users and their needs and wants? As the library literature legitimizes generational issues as reasons for behavior differences among library staff, I hope someone comes along with real solutions about how to move past the differences and really work together as a team without arbitrary conflicts based on age."

Other younger librarians also feel that these navel-gazing discussions are counterproductive, and that they even speak ill of their own generation's ability to lead in the future. Christine Kujawa, Head of Circulation Department/ Reference Librarian, Bismarck Veterans Memorial Public Library, Bismarck,

ND, says: "I've followed discussions of librarians who say they are in the 'next generation' group. They talk about why it's unfair that bosses don't let them show their tattoos or wear jeans at work. They aren't allowed to keep a beverage at the reference desk. They can't wear lip and tongue rings. I don't see myself as part of this group. I don't see these discussions as 'next generation' issues. As a professional librarian, I'm worried about other issues like intellectual freedom, funding for libraries, pay equity, and bridging the digital divide. I think about the future of leadership in our field. Who are the future leaders? Hopefully not someone who's worried about whether or not they can keep a cup of coffee at the reference desk and wear a tongue ring."

NextGens who have not yet spent significant time working in the profession may not yet have sufficient practical background to fully formulate their ideas about its future. Professional experience shows how theoretical ideas play out in practice, and both what our institutions are doing well, and where they fall short. If NextGens want to move beyond an immediate preoccupation with employment, they need to build a picture of what librarianship should look like. They need to empower themselves to realize that each voice is integral in moving the field forward. They need to articulate how fresh perspectives and ideas can build on existing professional foundations. As Christine Schutz, Library Director, Albertson College of Idaho, Caldwell, writes: "I want to kick my way out of the librarian 'box,' without losing the core meaning and function of what it means to be a librarian."

Ask the tough questions that define how the field will move forward. How can NextGens work to change the image of the profession? How do they help their colleagues convince taxpayers, deans, or corporate vice presidents of the need for continuing, let alone increasing, funding in an era of budget cuts, corporate belt-tightening, tax revolts, and the perception that everything is easily available online? Should NextGens fight for alternative funding models? Should they look at realistic ways to restructure their institutions? Should librarians continue to require the MLS for professional-level positions, or push for an alternative undergraduate degree or certification? In smaller libraries with one or no MLS personnel, what are some ways to move beyond day-to-day concerns and connect with the larger profession?

Be Part of the Solution

When libraries nationwide "restructure" and restaff with cheaper personnel, reduce hours, and cut positions to part-time, NextGens need to think about what they collectively can do to help resolve these issues. The difficulties that some report in finding sustainable entry-level employment are but one symptom of a larger issue; if there is to even be a profession in the future, we need to address these problems now. Libraries do not generally pay low salaries out of spite, but out of necessity. Libraries do not willfully cut positions; they make tough choices as best they can to work within their limited budgets.

Christina Stoll, Knowledge Management Specialist, North Suburban Library System, Wheeling, IL, notes: "Younger librarians also have to deal with uncertainty about how society views libraries and librarians. A library's value is currently being questioned more than when Baby Boomers entered the workplace. Younger librarians are being forced to relook at the entire library profession, and possibly reinvent it, so it remains a core part of our communities as it did 50 years ago."

Failure to move our profession forward leaves it completely subject to outside forces, or leaves NextGens stuck in stagnant institutions. Younger librarians can talk forever on lists, at conferences, and in person about what they want their institutions, associations, and profession to look like, but they need to put that talk into action by working to transform professional organizations and the overall professional outlook. They have the responsibility to incorporate a next generation perspective everywhere—from library workplaces, to conferences, to the professional literature. This can be accomplished in countless small ways, helping organizations evolve to meet changing needs. From setting up a simple IM account to handling incoming questions rather than investing in a cumbersome virtual reference infrastructure, to advocating for libraries from the perspective of users and decision makers rather than that of librarians themselves, different viewpoints and fresh ideas help move the profession forward.

Concerns about our professional future are not, of course, unique to NextGens, but they are the ones who will be dealing with the extended impact of current actions. What NextGens do now and over the course of the next decade or so builds the foundation of their professional future. Some under-40 survey respondents were also concerned that their older colleagues' fears about the profession's future can lead to concerns about younger librarians who seem to embody impending instability. One respondent wrote: "There is a lot of fear about the future of libraries, and that fear can translate to an attack on or defensiveness about young librarians. We're easy targets for that fear, because we embody the things that cause the anxiety, like love of technology, explorations of new directions for library service, and changing definitions of the profession." Another writes: "I would say that the issue is not always generational. It's bringing libraries and services into the next century and beyond. We need to change with the world, and libraries still move a bit too slowly for my taste, due to too many layers of bureaucracy and upper management."

Leadership

Even those not in a formal management position can take on leadership roles within their institutions; leadership qualities are not necessarily bound up in formal job titles or assignments. Look for quantifiable opportunities, such as chairing an internal committee, heading up a grant project, serving as a community liaison, or offering to take charge of an intern or volunteer. Look at where your leadership skills are strong, and where they might be lacking—make a conscious effort to shore up these areas. Leaders are those able to articulate a vision of the future and get others on board, whether in a small departmental project or an institutionwide initiative.

Katie Dunneback: "The Young Librarian"

What inspired you to create The Young Librarian Web site (www.younglibrarian.net) and Weblog (http://young librarian. blogspot.com), and why did you pick the name?

The Weblog is what started it all. It was mainly a place for me to post about my job search and what a pain in the butt it was turning out to be. I wanted to let other new librarians out there know that at least one other person was having a hard time finding a job. About two to three months into writing for the Weblog, I knew that I wanted it to be something more than just me kvetching about the job market. That's when I got the bright idea to expand into a Web site, and then I could keep practicing my HTML and CSS skills. I really enjoy writing, but those who have read my articles have probably gotten the idea that I'm not the most formal writer. I wanted to give people a place where they could explore topics of interest to new and young librarians, and get their feet wet in the publishing arena. There's this feature that I'd love to see take off called "A Day in the Life of a (Insert Job Title Here)," but we've only got one entry so far.

As for naming, I fell into the "pick an adjective and add librarian to the end" naming convention, and since I'm young for the field (mid/late-20s), I went with that.

What kind of response have you had to The Young Librarian?

Overall, I've had a very positive response to the Weblog and Web site. I did have one person leave a comment asking if I meant "young librarian" to be a joke, and another person responded in a similar face- tious manner. I just left them to joke around on their own. I hope to devote more time and energy to the Web site to take it to the next level, but it's going to depend on whether people want to have it as a resource. I cre- ated it in order to give other people an opportunity, but if they don't want to use it, I can't force them to.

In your opinion, what are the top challenges younger librarians currently face? What makes these unique to young librarians?

Wonderful question. I feel like a broken record because many of these issues have been discussed ad nauseum on e-mail lists and in the professional literature in the last few years. The low salaries affect us because many of us are single and are carrying a high debt-load due to student loans from a bachelor's and master's— often more than one master's—degree. Yes, many of us need to have the rose-colored glasses ripped from our faces when we begin new jobs, but when we face lack of professional respect from our co-workers, that drags us even further down. I think that the people who keep quoting the mythical librarian shortage is what is hurt- ing us the most. We enter this profession thinking that there are going to be decent paying full-time jobs for the picking. The cold hard slap of reality is greatly discouraging to many of us.

What do younger librarians have to offer the profession, and how can they increase their visibility and influence?

We offer fresh blood. Seriously, not to sound vampirish or anything, but we bring new enthusiasm for the profession to the table. Adaptation is what is going to help this profession survive into the future, and if you don't have enthusiasm for what you do, you will resist the adaptation. I think that the best way to increase their visibility and influence is to get involved in the various organizations, publish articles on topics dear to their hearts, and most of all, don't sit on their duffs! Like they say about elections, if you don't make your voice heard, don't complain about the state of things.

Do you have any other tips for your peers?

Anonymity is not a bad thing when you're venting about someone in particular if you care about your relationship with him or her. Anonymity is not guaranteed. Get involved, whether it's on committees in your library, running a Web site, writing articles, doing book reviews, or running for a board/council seat for one of the national organizations. You'll find your career, and yourself, much richer for it. Make friends outside the profession. Make friends inside the profession. Have a hobby outside of librarianship. Life is too damn short not to enjoy what you do.

Katie Dunneback, 27, is Reference Librarian at Westchester Public Library in Westchester, IL.

On the job, many NextGens soon realize the necessity of taking leadership roles on their own—and that in many cases they will lack institutional support. One survey respondent mentions the dichotomy between institutional lip service and reality: "I think I have been most surprised by the contradictory messages I have gotten at my first job (and that seem to be fairly rampant in the profession as a whole). Right out of school, new librarians are asked to have a large amount of experience, knowledge, and ability and are asked to step up and take leadership roles while in their entry-level positions. However, once in the job, there seems to often be a lack of mentoring, a lack of assistance in developing leadership skills, and a general sense of dismissal as far as the skills/ability/knowledge the new person has. They want you to have a lot of experience to get a job but then don't value that experience once you get the job, and they want you to take initiative and lead without helping you get to a place where you feel comfortable doing so." (Find more on taking advantage of and creating leadership opportunities in Chapter 5.)

If you have ideas of ways to move your department, section, or institution forward, part of being a leader is accompanying these thoughts with practical discussion of how your ideas can be accomplished. Become known as someone who offers constructive solutions and follows through on projects, and opportunities will soon find you.

Issues

The following brief discussions of several issues affecting the direction of our profession offer more questions than answers. These are examples of issues worth working on or developing a coherent NextGen perspective on, so that NextGens together can work on moving the profession forward. These issues are, of course, not unique to next generation librarians; older colleagues have done and continue to do fantastic work. NextGens need to build on and respect what has already been done. As Portland, OR, MLS student Kevin Moore notes: "The new generation has much to offer the future of librarianship, but we also have much to learn from our elders. They have been where we are and have years of experience dealing with issues similar to what we face—in fact, they are facing those issues right now. Fortunately, their experience informs them of pitfalls and of practices that have succeeded in the past. The challenges posed by budgetary restraints, social fears, and technology are not new to the profession. How librarians have dealt with them in the past can teach us how to deal with them in the present and future."

Budget Cuts

Libraries across the country are fighting for recognition and funding in an era of tax cuts, budgetary constraints, funding crises, and increased serials, benefits, and other costs, as well as competition with other agencies. If

NextGens lack libraries to work in, they lack much of a future. Those interested in tracking such problems can look at "endangered libraries" at http://librarydust.typepad.com/library_dust/2005/01/endangered_libr.html, as well as at ALA's library funding page at www.ala.org/ala/news/library funding/libraryfunding.htm. When NextGens read basic professional literature such as *American Libraries* and *Library Journal,* they are confronted with a never-ending litany of libraries that have lost funding and have been forced to cut staff and close branches. While some institutions are doing well (and have the money to do very interesting things) others are cutting staff via attrition, offering branches staffed entirely by lower-paid paraprofessionals, or closing entirely.

These budget cuts and warning signs also tie in with associations' current recruitment efforts. ACRL's Ad Hoc Task Force on Salaries and Recruitment, for one, points out the current U.S. parallels to the Canadian situation in the 1990s. "Volatile budget environments and major cuts in operating expenditures were common in Canada throughout the decade. Many Canadian libraries were forced to give up positions in order to fund budget cuts, to keep positions open, or to fund only temporary or contract appointments as service demands warranted. Few positions were filled on a permanent basis except for those deemed highly strategic (e.g., IT librarians). Some Canadian librarians speak of the 'lost generation of library school graduates,' those graduates of MLIS programs who drifted from contract to contract or moved out of Canada to practice their profession."[2] As a result, some Canadian libraries are now having trouble filling middle management positions because of a lack of people to move up the ranks, cannot meet demands in service, and have lost out on the professional vitality of an entire generation. How can we avoid having a similar scenario play out here? Are we seeing the early warning signs now?

Budgetary problems, further, go hand-in-hand with salary issues. Should librarians be looking at large-scale unionization, à la teachers? Should we turn our efforts toward marketing our institutions, or toward transforming them into something else altogether? Under-40 survey respondent James Loyd, Head of Children's Department, Decatur Public Library, AL, says succinctly that "one of our biggest problems is apathy and/or ignorance on the part of agencies that control funding." Should NextGens throw their efforts into organizations such as ALA/APA? What kind of collective action can they take to protest library cuts and help realign budgetary priorities?

Many libraries are in competition for funding with other services, and, if libraries and librarians are not perceived as essential, they become an easy target for cuts. The perception that "everything is online" only exacerbates this. People are willing to fund libraries the amount they perceive they are worth; the challenge is to change that perception and to demonstrate value. As for our low salaries, comparing ourselves to other professions and to what their members make is not helpful unless we look at concrete steps that other professionals took to change perceptions. Other historically low-paid, traditionally women's professions such as teaching and nursing have made great progress. Part of the librarians' problem lies in our professional fragmentation. Public school teachers, for example, are unionized, but also are an easily-defined block and have continuing education/certification and other requirements that most librarians lack; librarians are split up among various types and have widely varying positions, titles, and responsibilities.

One under-40 survey respondent notes that: "We have to sell ourselves. It is so easy for there to be misperceptions that we do not add value to the world of information or that we are not needed because of the Internet. I think most of us get into this field because of a deep love of libraries (trust me, I'm not doing it for the huge paycheck ...), and I think sometimes it doesn't occur to us that libraries are a good that needs to be 'sold' to the larger world." Another says that: "I believe a 'next generation librarian' is also defined by a strong public service ethic. In my opinion, outreach and promotion of library services is becoming one of the most important parts of our jobs." Leigh Ann DePope, Library Director, Seaford District Library, DE, agrees: "The most pressing issue facing our profession today is learning how to be flexible in a rapidly and ever-changing electronic environment within the same financial and personal constraints. We can no longer sit arranging our books and analyzing our circulation stats when our patrons are leaving us for the coffeehouse down the street. This is a multitasking, instant-access, spur-of-the-moment communication society, and libraries need to kick up the horsepower if we want to stay on board."

Peter Bromberg, Program Development Coordinator, South Jersey Regional Library Cooperative, Gibbsboro, NJ, lists his top issues as: "1) Remaining relevant. That means offering services that people want, in the way they want them. This includes everything from story time to virtual reference. This means listening to our customers and paying attention to trends in our culture (e.g., the trend to immediate connection through hand-held devices; premium on convenience and satisficing); 2) Creating welcoming and inviting spaces that customers will want to use (see www.sjrlc.org/tradingspaces/), and; 3) Communicating our relevance (marketing)." Take the time to demonstrate libraries' economic and life-changing impact to decision makers.

Remaining viable also implies making money-saving changes that allow libraries to provide service within budgetary constraints; NextGens can come up with some exciting ideas in this area. Several survey respondents stressed the importance of cooperation and collaboration. Nanette Donohue, Technical Services Manager, Champaign Public Library, IL, explains: "I also think that NextGens, as a whole, are cooperative. Many of us are used to working cooperatively from a very young age—cooperative learning was an educational trend/buzzword during our formative years, so we grew up working together. Our ability to work cooperatively will pay off in this era of limited funding, because working together, we will be able to provide the services our patrons need." Analiza Perez, a student at Texas Woman's University, Denton, agrees: "There is a certain fearlessness when it comes to technology and cooperative endeavors that really separates my generation from the 40-plus generation. At a time when budget cuts really take a toll on all types of libraries, efficiency in the workplace aided by technology and the ability to join together with other libraries will be the main forces that allow libraries to thrive."

Technology

Those who have grown up with gadgets can be especially susceptible to the "new and cool" syndrome, lusting for technology for technology's sake rather than first seeing how it fits into their libraries' missions, culture, and patron expectations. Temper a NextGen appreciation for technology with an understanding of which technologies truly improve service to patrons; find ways to remain near the edge without falling over. Amy Phillips, Reference Librarian, Philip S. Miller Library, Douglas County Libraries, Castle Rock, CO, explains: "We are more often jumping into things without considering all of the ramifications ... We also may not be as sympathetic as we could be to our older co-workers who don't deal with technological change as well." Younger librarians also need to remain connected to older patrons and their varying technological comfort levels and needs as long-time librarians retire.

A number of NextGen survey respondents recognize that their own technological assumptions sometimes hamper effective service to patrons. Vanessa J. Morris, Adult/Teen Librarian, Free Library of Philadelphia, PA, explains: "I find that veteran librarians are more patient and accommodating to patrons, whereas current-day librarians have higher expectations of the literacy of patrons and thus are less patient with various degrees of illiteracy (i.e., computer illiteracy)." Over-40 respondents share similar concerns about their younger colleagues and technology. One says: "I welcome their insight as to what sorts of services younger people want and expect. However, lots and lots of public library patrons are older (moms with kids, retired folks), so I think that it is important that the under-40 librarians are respectful when they provide services. I've seen people in their 50s struggle with a mouse, because they just haven't had to use one before."

There is a widespread perception that younger librarians, especially Millennials, have a natural facility with technology from having grown up with it. Don Tapscott sums this view up by saying: "What makes this generation different from all others before it? It is the first to grow up surrounded by digital media."[3] Some over-40 survey respondents are excited about the technological savvy of their younger colleagues. Janine Reid, Executive Director, Weld Library District, Greeley, CO, says: "Technosavvy from the get-go. Yeah! Technology forms the foundation of our work. It has been a real challenge for the past 20 years to get 'old-school' librarians up to speed. The newer librarians don't come with the technophobe baggage." Cindy Mielke, Library Director, Goodall City Library, Ogallala, NE, agrees: "Younger librarians have an advantage of a lifelong exposure to technology, while those of us who are older were exposed to technology as adults. It is easier to learn as a youth. They don't have the hesitance factor."

The assumption of technological proficiency is common among NextGen librarians themselves; under-40 survey respondents say:

➤ "We know computers. We love computers. We grew up with computers. We use computers at home, not just at work. We have an instinct about computers—don't just use programs by rote."

➤ "Overall, I would say that although many older librarians are comfortable with technology, there are those who are not, whereas virtually all NextGen librarians, particularly the ones who are now in their teens and twenties, have grown up with technology, and are comfortable with using it and learning new ways to apply it."

➤ "It's an understanding of modernity, in a way. I grew up with video games and VCRs; I was in college when the Internet became a research tool (thus introducing the

Internet as an integral part of my understanding of research); I've never needed to carry on a correspondence by paper mail … it's simply a difference of experience and understanding of the world."

➤ "I grew up with computers in school and am very comfortable learning new systems, which are constantly changing. My older colleagues usually seem to experience duress when faced with learning a new system or a new version of a system."

➤ "I think we bring a technical savvy, or ability to quickly learn and effectively use new technologies as they emerge. It seems like we're more willing to implement them while some older librarians are content with their current technologies regardless of what the newer ones add in terms of value, ease of use, etc."

➤ "I entered librarianship already feeling comfortable with using computers and the Internet. While the generation before me had to adapt to this, my generation is used to this and will have to adapt to the future technology that emerges."

➤ "I think I have a different perspective on librarianship and libraries as I have grown up in the computer generation, I've had a home computer since I started grade school, and never passed in a paper that wasn't word processed. I've also never really learned how to use a card catalog; instead I feel very comfortable with using any kind of online catalog."

➤ "We grew up with computers, and later on the Internet. Given the impact technology is having and will continue to have on libraries, that experience and natural aptitude will become invaluable."

➤ "I think technological expertise is one of the most important qualities that NextGen librarians have. Most of us grew up with technology. For those of us on the older end of the spectrum, it was the Atari 2600 and the Apple IIe. The younger NextGens reminisce about the NES and

Windows 3.1. Regardless, technology has always been an intimate part of NextGen librarians' lives—many of us have never really lived without it. This really gives us an opportunity to shine among colleagues who may not have the sorts of experiences we have."

Some, though, fail to think about the long history of technology and its use in libraries—a few over-40 survey respondents point out that they have been using computers for years, and that, in some cases, the fact that they learned to use technology when it was less "user-friendly" gives them a deeper ability to go under the hood and to understand how and why things work as they do. Others are concerned about younger colleagues' assumptions about their technological illiteracy. Patricia Coffie, Director, Waverly Public Library, IA, says: "When building this second building, I had to take some aside and say 'Have had my own computer since the Commodore 64 and currently have what is described as a 'screaming machine'; routinely read three books a week, subscribe to and read three newspapers. Have already built another library building. Have some understanding of libraries and library service. You can talk to me about computers, snow removal, wiring, cabling, color, shape, and, most of all, *function*.' " One under-40 survey respondent also notes: "Having trained all ages of librarians in the use of library automation, I have realized that though it may be widely true that younger librarians may corner the market on technological awareness and abilities, some of the people putting information technology to its best uses are older librarians who know libraries."

Further, technology is a changing target. The technology NextGens grew up using 10 or 15 years ago is not the same technology that libraries currently must adapt and respond to. Regardless of age or year of graduation, we all have the same need for ongoing professional development and current awareness. In the early 1990s, the common technological assumption was that CD-ROM was the wave of the future in libraries. In 2005, no one would make that assumption. Pay attention to trends, and be willing to jettison or revise your assumptions as the technological tide keeps moving.

One survey respondent says, "Even at 28, I'm rapidly losing that edge … I'm starting to see students who are more computer-literate than I am, and the Internet, particularly distance education tools, is rapidly changing the education landscape." Others, though, see lifelong learning as a natural skill for NextGens who have grown up with changing technology. Lauren Pressley, MLS student, UNC-Greensboro, NC, explains: "We're used to learning new information quickly. When our cell phone contract runs out every year and we get a new phone, we learn the new cell phone operating system. When iPods and other MP3 players came out, we rushed to learn how to use them to take our music collection anywhere. We quickly learned the language of instant messaging and file sharing. Librarians need to be able to pick up new information on the fly, and this generation is so used to doing it that we don't often even think of this as a unique skill."

The assumption of digital fluency also ignores the issue of the digital divide, although this may be less of an issue by the time people have graduated from library school. The assumption of technological expertise and excitement, though, as well as the experience of having grown up with technology, has the capacity to help transform library workplaces and institutions. When an entering generation has a tendency toward fluency in one area where its members naturally become teachers and leaders, this contributes to the flattening of workplace hierarchies and shows that we can all learn from one another. One under-40 survey respondent notes: "I sometimes get frustrated at the lack of computer literacy exhibited by some of my older colleagues (I have to explain to them how to do things that are second-nature to me), but, on the other hand, it is nice to have something that I can give to them in return for the knowledge and advice they have given me."

Education

Library education, as mentioned in Chapter 2, is in a period of transition. One issue: Do librarians continue to advocate for the primacy of the MLS, or do we work to define alternative career paths or certification opportunities for library workers without degrees, or an alternative BA degree to serve as the entry-level qualification? Some non-MLS under-40 survey respondents, in particular, see the divide between librarians with and without degrees as a generational issue in itself: "Though there are lots of older librarians who are very happy to have younger blood in the profession, there are still those who look down their nose at those of us who don't have the MLS ('outsiders')." The previously mentioned ACRL Ad Hoc Task Force on Recruitment and Retention Issues makes note of the increased skills and specialization of many non-MLS library workers, pointing to this as a reason fewer qualified individuals are choosing to move into paraprofessional positions, which in many libraries have limited career paths.[4] This points to the need to work on defining career paths and opportunities for all library workers.

Others mention the need to earn the MLS as a deterrent to new entrants, especially when the profession is trying to attract younger members. Jan Kuebel, for one, names among her priorities "developing a viable BS/SLIS program. With more and more students being introduced to and retained in libraries, or entranced with the computers, as the case may be, we must present our profession as a vibrant, enlightening profession. Imagine this, if you will: A high school student has to select a profession to investigate and report on. He chooses to write about being a librarian, because he spends more time in the library after school than anywhere else. He feels comfortable with the YA librarian, because she helps him with those last-minute book reports. During his research, he hears that he must complete six years of college to become a librarian, with four of those six years [spent] studying another profession. Confusing? Yes. Deterring? Undoubtedly." This also adds another dimension to salary issues, as many NextGens' concerns involve the extra education (and loans) involved in getting the MLS and the relatively low perceived return on that investment when compared to other professions that simply require the BA. On a related note, next generation librarians' struggle for respect and to be heard within their institutions and the larger field should increase their empathy for and connection to nondegreed parapros engaged in similar struggles. Perhaps the library of the future can have more harmonious relations because of such connections.

Alternative or undergraduate credentials are more of an issue, though, in academic libraries where librarians work with faculty members that place primacy on graduate degrees. Requiring a bachelor's degree in library or information science and a subject-specific master's for some academic positions, though, might combine well to allow non-MLS librarians to liaison with specific departments and retain their respect.

Regarding the MLS itself, what are the best ways to transform library school curricula so that they prepare new grads to work in 21st-century libraries, while still providing a strong foundation in professional principles and traditional skills? Are library schools maintaining the proper standards, or focusing more on turning out large numbers of graduates to help remedy a future professional shortage? Some under-40 survey respondents see the need for a different professorial mix or focus: "It is ironic that we are being taught (for the most part) by people who are of the older generation. This is good because it gives good perspective, but at the same time, it doesn't adequately prepare us for the future or current changes. It's best to have a mix of older and younger professors."

Privacy and Intellectual Freedom

A number of survey respondents mentioned privacy and intellectual freedom issues as among the most pressing currently affecting the profession. The USA PATRIOT Act, CIPA, DMCA and other recent legislation have spotlighted a disturbing trend toward tightening controls. Echoing many, Kevin Moore lists among his main issues "intellectual freedom. Paranoia has found legislative form in the USA PATRIOT Act and CIPA, threatening to invade patron privacy and turn librarians into thought police." Libraries and librarians across the country are subject to ever-stricter controls and ever-increasing challenges. Some administrations and Boards add to such concerns with a rush to jump on technologies such as RFID (radio frequency indentification) or even fingerprinting library patrons who wish to use the Internet.

One over-40 survey respondent wishes to tell NextGen colleagues: "… don't let anyone minimize your professional standards: You are responsible for maintaining a conduit for the free flow of information, a vital system of democratic dialogue and action. You may spend most of your day checking out Danielle Steel books, but stay familiar with what else is on your shelves and accessible from your Web site. Make sure the important stuff stays there, as well."

Hand-in-hand with information literacy goes the understanding of what people are giving up by complying with greater controls. Adriana Edwards-Johnson, Serials, Electronic Collections, and Technical Processing Librarian, Southwestern Oklahoma State University, Weatherford, explains: "I also think literacy is a major issue. Literacy involves so much more than reading and writing. Librarians must strive with other professionals to promote comprehension of what people are reading. Censorship, book challenges, filters, and all the like could almost be eradicated if the public understood what they were reading and had a more global view of actions." Follow sites like FreeCulture.org (http://free culture.org) and blogs like Lawrence Lessig's (www.lessig.org/blog/) for more on these issues.

Making Yourself Heard

Most comfortable in the company of their peers, many next generation librarians tend to save their best energy and input for online discussion lists like nexgenlib-l and NEWLIB-L. Unfortunately, interacting only in NextGen and new librarian venues means that you are preaching to the choir. How do NextGens get their voices heard by the larger library community, especially by decision makers?

A number of younger librarians are frustrated by the perception that their opinions are automatically discounted due to their age. One writes: "My age (21) is among the lowest I've met so far of practicing professionals. At once it allows me greater access to the young people with whom I work (both patrons and the young members of the nonlibrarian staff) and limits the amount my voice can be heard among other professionals. In this profession, sheer years of experience count for a lot." Develop a sense of your own self-worth and build on small successes. The best way to get heard is to prove that you have something to say that is worth listening to.

Others feel that their perspectives as younger librarians are summarily discounted because they are seen as a threat to their more-established colleagues. Another respondent to the under-40 survey says: "I have a unique perspective on users, technology, change management, and the future of the profession that many of my older colleagues cannot understand or find very intimidating. I AM different than they are."

To bring your own voice to the larger profession, think about writing for publications, giving conference presentations or poster sessions, or starting a relevant Web site or blog. Again, here, think about your potential audience and who you want to reach. Be willing to take on new, different, or even controversial topics. Think about the best way to approach and reach an audience made up of multiple generations and points of view. As Michelle Millet, Information Literacy Coordinator, Trinity University, San Antonio, TX, says: "But we have all bonded, in this weird sort of way, by all of this talk about our generation. All of a sudden, people are noticing us and paying attention to what we have to say, and we have to seize that moment!"

Ria Newhouse

Can you talk a little bit about what prompted you to survey new librarians on their experiences, and briefly summarize the results?

I graduated from the University of Illinois at Urbana-Champaign with my MLS (or MS in Library Science, actually) in May 2002 and promptly found a job as a

Teen Services Librarian in a public library. April Spisak, my close friend and colleague from grad school, had graduated in August 2001 and accepted a position in Children's Services in a public library. We found ourselves talking on the phone one day after we had both graduated, commiserating about the profession—we felt like we had been promised great things—we were librarians, after all! But our experiences didn't reflect the intellectual freedom-fighting machines that we had been told we could become while in grad school. The day-to-day issues of working in libraries, with other librarians, were very different from what we expected. So, after discussing the merits, problems, and surprises in librarianship for weeks on end, we decided we had a matter worthy of research on our hands. We kept asking ourselves: Are we the only ones who feel this way? Is everyone else happy? We decided to take the issue "to the streets" and do a survey. And everything just grew from there.

We issued a survey in 2003 to NextGen librarians and sent the survey to several lists: nexgenlib-l, PUBYAC, REFLIB, and Child Lit. One hundred twenty-four people responded to the survey, and shared both qualitative and quantitative responses to our questions. We asked people about their experiences in their library school programs: Did they feel prepared to be a librarian when they graduated? (55 percent did.) We asked people if they felt happy in their workplaces. (57 percent were strongly happy.) We wanted to know if people felt like they had become "librarians for life"—did they plan to stay in this career? (61 percent did.) And, most importantly, we asked respondents if they felt like libraries were open and affirming places for new librarians— almost 58 percent said yes, but the qualitative responses cracked open a chasm of responses that really got us going.

In short, we figured out very quickly that some of the problems we were having weren't just about us—

the problems were reflected in our generation and in our colleagues. We wanted to do something with our research; we took a leap of faith and applied to do a program at PLA [Public Library Association] in Seattle, and took off from there.

What reaction have you had to your presentations and Library Journal *article on the subject?*

The reactions have been mostly positive. After presentations, people will come up to us and thank us for talking about the issues that really need to be talked about and for saying the hard things that need to be said (and we do say some pretty hard—and harsh—things). Generation Xers will say: "That's exactly my experience—thanks for talking about it." Not many people have had an entirely negative reaction, but we have had people indicate that we should "suck it up" and deal with it because they had to go through it and, now, so do we. This is hilarious, since that's one of the things we address in presentations—that things don't need to be done the way they've always been done. Only a few people have been overtly hostile, saying that we're not willing to "pay our dues" or listen to wisdom. There wasn't a ton of response to the *Library Journal* article, but the responses we did get were generally positive.

You and your co-author April Spisak presented your findings to the ALA Executive Board at Annual 2004. Please explain how that happened. What was the Board's reaction?

April and I were asked to present to the Executive Board of the American Library Association at the 2004 Annual Conference in Orlando, Florida. It was a really big deal for us; we were both very excited and very, very nervous. Mary Ghikas, the Senior Associate Executive Director for ALA, had attended our presentation at PLA in Seattle and approached us afterward about presenting at ALA and for the Executive Board. We were, of course, thrilled. We spent countless hours preparing for the presentation and in all, had about 15 minutes to tell the biggest people in ALA about our generation—what we want, what we do, and how we feel.

The presentation part went fairly well and I only noticed a few eyes being rolled, heads being tossed, etc. There was a brief amount of time for questions after the presentation and most board members were kind to us. We were, after all, very critical (at times) about librarianship, ALA, and articles in *American Libraries*. Some people on the Executive Board simply didn't want to hear what we had to say, which we expected, but we never expected the response to be so blatant. One person on the board actually said "Just shut up!" This wasn't very heartening!

However, I have gone on to have really nice relationships with several board members and one of them is someone I consider a very close mentor. In the end, the experience was a good one and I think it helped make me a stronger librarian. It's hard to get up in front of the big names in ALA and identify problems—people never want to hear about problems—but we did it, and I'm proud of that.

What impact do you think your work has had?

I think April and I "hit" on this issue at exactly the right time. The generational clash has been a big issue in libraries, and I'm glad that we were able to identify and talk about that issue, but I feel like the bigger issue is really about recruitment, retention, and honesty. Our research sort of morphed from "What are the problems?" to "What are some solutions?" and "How can we keep talking about these issues, but change things as well?" April and I are no longer "new librarians," although we're still billed that way when we do presentations. It's now time for us (and our GenX and Millennial colleagues) to take these issues and change the outcomes.

When I think about outcomes and impacts, I think we've managed to identify an important issue to a lot of people—not enough, but a lot. We've managed to put a face on the younger side of librarianship and we are

> (speaking of my generation) adding our voices to ALA and librarianship in general. I think we're really changing the face of librarianship, as well, and the way things are done and will be done in the future. We've also managed to piss off a few people along the way, which is probably a good thing.
>
> **Ria Newhouse, 27, is Reference and Instruction Librarian at Metropolitan State University in Saint Paul, MN.**

Further, how do you make yourself heard in your own institution? Learning how to speak up—at meetings, to your supervisor, to your Board—and gaining others' attention is a learned skill. Newer and younger librarians face the added hurdle of many established librarians taking them less seriously. They need to combat these perceptions from the outset, not to confirm them by being timid or presenting ideas that are less than thought through. Realize that you need to take these opportunities for yourself, and not wait to have your opinions actively solicited. Think about how best to appeal to your colleagues' interests—and self-interest—when explaining how your ideas can benefit them and the institution.

Where To Now?

Where to from here? What happens as next generation librarians are challenged by "next-next" generation librarians? Remain connected to the reasons you went into the profession, and actively seek out opportunities to mentor others. (For more on this, see the comments from GenX librarians in Chapter 1 and the mentoring section in Chapter 7.) Mentoring others can reenergize you as well, reminding you of the enthusiasm you first brought to this profession and bringing you the viewpoints of generations to follow. Pay it forward, honoring those who have helped you along the way.

NextGens also need to work on broadening out of the librarian niche and connecting with the larger society. Under-40 survey respondent Heather Clark, Collection Management Librarian, Denver Seminary, Carey S. Thomas Library, CO, explains: "We need to integrate with the other information professions, which are emerging outside the traditional environments (e.g., knowledge management). We can learn so much from one another. I would like to see more willingness to reach out and less defensiveness of 'library territory' in our rhetoric."

As you move up in the library field or settle comfortably into a long-term position, remembering the experiences around your entry into the profession can help you relate to the experiences of generations to follow. Some over-40 survey respondents reflected on how quickly things change, as Beth Wheeler Dean, Head of Youth Services, Huntsville Madison County Public Library, Huntsville, AL, explains: "I now feel like one of the old guard instead of the 'whippersnappers.' In truth, I liked being the one that questioned the old ways."

Endnotes

1. Anne A. Salter, "Wanted—New Creations: Dinosaurs Need Not Apply," in Karl Bridges, ed., *Expectations of Librarians in the 21st Century*, Westport, CT: Greenwood, 2003: 53.
2. Association of College and Research Libraries (ACRL), Ad Hoc Task Force on Recruitment & Retention Issues, *Recruitment, Retention, and Restructuring: Human Resources in Academic Libraries*, Chicago: ALA, 2002: 7. See also Stanley J. Wilder, *Demographic Change in Academic Librarianship*, Washington, DC: ARL, 2003: xv.
3. Don Tapscott, *Growing Up Digital: The Rise of the Net Generation,* New York: McGraw-Hill, 1998: 1.
4. ACRL: 53.

A Note to Library Administrators

Alienating Generation X librarians with pedantic rules and no opportunities for growth and creativity will contribute to an organization fading away like a dinosaur. Instead managers will be challenged to direct their enthusiasm and lack of bureaucratic patience in a direction consistent with overall organizational objectives, and nurture a staff blending and knowledge sharing based on mutual respect and shared vision.

Pixey Anne Mosley[1]

If you have picked up this book as a library administrator interested in finding out where your GenX and GenY employees are coming from, or as a Boomer librarian interested in better relating to or interacting more productively with your younger colleagues, the preceding chapters have likely given you some insight into NextGen librarians' main concerns. Think now: How many of your library's mid-level managers will be retiring over the next few years? How many of your long-time employees? Do you have plans in place now for mentoring and building up new leaders, as well as for encouraging your current staff members to pass on their accumulated wisdom and institutional memory?

Find more in Chapter 1 on librarianship as an aging profession. Librarianship, though, is not only aging—librarians are older as a group than those in comparable professions, creating the upcoming need to replace retirees with vibrant new professionals. As Stanley J. Wilder, author of *Demographic Change in Academic Librarianship*, explains: "The management issue resulting from the aging of librarianship is not retirement; it is how to obtain new entrants in sufficient numbers, with quality and expertise, to replace retirees and keep the cycle turning."[2]

Beyond the need to ensure your institution's—and the profession's—future, it is costly to lose and to rehire and retrain employees. If multiple positions in your institution, and in other institutions, begin opening up as Baby Boomers start retiring in greater numbers, how attractive will your workplace be when librarians are more in demand and can be more choosy about their positions? Paying attention to retention is beneficial in both the short and long term. Start as early as the hiring and orientation process to train and mentor new employees.

Library administrators and managers concerned about an upcoming shortage of librarians, succession planning in their own institutions, and/or the future of the profession, would do well to think about ways to retain, encourage, and mentor the current generation of younger librarians. This may not be possible without paying special attention to the "big three" issues affecting many NextGens' commitment to the profession: a lack of entry-level opportunities, a lack of sustainable salaries, and a lack of opportunity to be a full participant in the profession. Avoid falling into stereotypes such as "all younger librarians are whiners," and think about the reasons and realities behind their concerns.

As the ACRL Committee on Retention and Recruitment explains: "With a significant percentage of academic librarians planning to retire in the next decade and declining numbers of MLIS graduates and job applicants to academic libraries, retaining those current professionals takes on new importance. Such individuals not only need to be retained, but also need to be mentored, coached, and developed for future leadership roles in the academic library community."[3] This is important in all types of libraries, not just academic institutions.

Our Professional Future

Throughout this book, you have heard the words of younger librarians who are frustrated by their inability to find a job, their inability to pay back excessive student loans on a paltry entry-level salary, or their administrations' commitments to excessive bureaucracy and fear of change. An alarming number of under-40 survey respondents said they had already considered leaving the profession, some after merely a couple of years in frustrating entry-level positions, some after earning their MLS and being unable to find a position in the field, and some after trying to live for a while on an entry-level salary. Others talked about leaving their employers for other libraries that offered more opportunity. Their comments included such common themes as:

➤ "There are many areas that value the degree I have and have better pay. While I didn't go into the profession for money, one needs to be paid enough to survive. Librarians are still paid as if we were all housewives [just looking for] something to do, and as if our income didn't matter."

➤ "Absolutely [I'd consider leaving]. Because I don't feel like my drive and talents are valued by my employers or my field in general."

➤ "Younger librarians will not be content to stay in one location for 30-plus years. And if employers want them to, then there will need to be a larger drive to increase continuing education opportunities. Boomers were demanding in what they wanted from employers—but tended to put up with difficult situations; younger librarians will demand better and will not stick around if situations don't improve."

➤ "Keep newer librarians engaged so that they don't leave the profession. Recruitment is pointless without retention."

➤ "I'm young enough that I can train in another field/switch careers, thus I don't feel fully invested in the profession or committed to it; it's my choice at this point to stay in librarianship. When the bottom falls out of academic librarianship, I don't have to worry about whether I'll find a job in another library because I'm far from retirement age. I don't have children either, and this gives me more professional options as well."

➤ "I often considered leaving the profession and trying out another field. Why? Well, during my long job hunt, of course! It becomes so frustrating to work so hard—get the degrees, do the internships, volunteer in libraries, work part-time for over six years in libraries—and yet not land a position. Yet my friends in other fields who have much less experience in their fields are landing jobs. And my older colleagues from library school who again, have much less experience in libraries, are having no trouble finding a job. Hmmm … I felt something was definitely up."

➤ "Yes. The pay for a public librarian is nil. It's tough in today's economy."

➤ "In previous positions, there was a very unhealthy work environment. Coming home crying or working 50 hours a week does not make a happy librarian. However, I did something about it and moved on to the next job. Now, I have perspective."

➤ "I think something else that makes younger librarians' situations unique is that we're supporting ourselves on a librarian's salary and possibly a family, too. Unlike some librarians from the Baby Boomers' generation, we don't have spouses with well-paying jobs. This isn't a way to pass the time. It's a job to pay the bills. And it is becoming more and more difficult to do so."

➤ "My age makes me uncomfortable with the profession. The profession is designed for women who are planning to work part-time, don't need benefits, and aren't the primary wage-earners in their families. Younger librarians aren't looking for that type of job. We're more empowered."

➤ "I currently feel a great need to leave the library profession and pursue a course that will allow me to provide for my family, but my co-workers are the best group of people with which I have ever worked."

➤ "Due to the negative ageist environment, many younger people have been dissuaded from entering or continuing in the profession, and when the time comes when the current librarians retire, there will be no one to fill in the empty spaces."

➤ "I would love to find part-time professional work, but where I'm at, I'm lucky if I can find part-time library work and then it doesn't pay enough to cover child care. I'm not working in the field right now because the [nonlibrary] job I have pays enough to cover child care."

➤ "The issue of recruitment and retention continues to be stressed amongst the library associations, but they refuse to see the disconnect. Bottom line—the disconnect is between salaries that currently exist and what they should be, as well as an environment of status quo. Risk taking is a real big issue, one which needs to be addressed and encouraged."

➤ "If I can, I try to discourage anyone from entering the profession."

➤ "Most librarians have resigned themselves to mediocrity, and it has made me very angry to see the profession as it truly is, scared for its life and with good reason (not how the library faculty make it sound, as a profession on the brink of a renaissance). I don't know if the renaissance will ever come, and if I got a chance to get out of this profession, I would take it and never look back. I know many new librarians who are perfectly happy in the profession, and I'm glad for them. I want more, though. I chose poorly."

➤ "I graduated really excited about this field and determined to find work in an academic or special library, but I reached the point where I was applying for a wide variety of jobs (researcher, privacy officer, writer, etc.) that were only tangentially related to library science. I am happily employed in a special library now, and intend to stay for the foreseeable future, but I no longer have a firm commitment to being a librarian until I retire, because I will benefit more by being more flexible about my career options."

➤ "[I have thought of moving] to a field where I don't feel like I'm being replaced by a computer, where everything isn't political, where I am needed to do actual work instead of troubleshooting Word for eight hours a day. And a field I can go home at the end of the day and not have to care. And, oh yes, get paid enough to live on."

These comments—and these are only a representative sample—should scare anyone interested in the future of our profession.

On the bright side, younger librarians do, as a whole, love the profession, and share similar reasons for choosing librarianship as their older peers. Reasons they mention include:

➤ "I love books. I love reading them, and I love organizing them. I love helping people find what they want; it's just such a wonderful feeling."

➤ "The ability to access information and disseminate it to a public who really need it. Helping people is my reward. As a trainer, I help staff better understand the big picture of the library mission. In my role as a reference librarian, I share the gifts of our library resources with the public."

➤ "I've always loved finding information and the field incorporates many of my skill sets. I was also seeking an intellectually stimulating environment, one in which I wouldn't be in 'the rat race.' "

➤ "I want to serve and I feel that librarians/libraries offer an excellent service. I love being able to help customers find information and I learn something new every day."

➤ "I appreciated being able to combine my desire to help people with a reason to learn about everything."

➤ "The truth is—I love libraries. I love the fact that in my checkered career path, I was able to go to the library to learn the things I needed to land better jobs. I love the fact that they are open to all, one of our few real, noncommercial public spaces. I see so much potential for libraries—we are the organizers of information, and what are we in but the information age? I also think that I have the ability to really tell the story of libraries, to advocate for libraries. I see knowledge as so important to our society and our future—and libraries hold the accumulated knowledge of our civilization."

➤ "What I love about library science is that no day is ever the same, and you learn new things every day. When doing reference, it's all the fun of research without having to actually write the paper; when doing cataloging, it's like being paid to do puzzles all day. The more I study and the more I learn about LIS, the more interesting I find it. There is no limit to the things I can learn every day."

➤ "Librarianship chose me. I'm a child that books built. I've been raised in libraries. I believe in the power of the printed word. I'm dedicated to service. I believe that, together with teachers, librarians are the world's guardians of culture, literacy, and education."

➤ "To provide and preserve access to information to all."

➤ "I decided to enter the field because it is the only career that seemed to meld perfectly with my own generalized knowledge base. I know a little bit about everything, and I love to find out more. As a librarian and research teacher, I get to learn more every day, and not all in one subject!"

Some survey respondents express conflicted sentiments about their love for the profession and its ideals, in contrast with their concerns about practices in their particular institutions or about the field's future.

While most over-40 survey respondents were of the opinion that younger librarians would stay in the profession if it were their true calling, others express concerns about their younger colleagues leaving for better opportunities. As one says: "Yes, I am concerned about younger librarians not even entering the field, let alone leaving it after they've spent all that time and money for an MLS. When they get in and find out what we already know, I don't think they're going to hang around waiting for things to improve." Martha Vaughn, Librarian, Girls Preparatory School, Chattanooga, TN, concurs: "Yes, I'm concerned about younger librarians leaving the field. Just yesterday I learned about a young man who is considering going to law school right after he finishes his MLS. He's scared that he's chosen to go into a dying field where there are severe cuts, layoffs, and extremely poor morale. The public library in our own community is in severe financial difficulty and, of course, the news from Buffalo is devastating!"

Your Professional Responsibilities

So, how do you—as a manager, administrator, or concerned professional—encourage, recruit, assist, and retain younger staff? Some might
wish to take a page from *Library Journal's* Librarian of the Year 2005, North
Carolina State University Director of Libraries, Susan Nutter, who reserves
certain positions at the NCSU Libraries for new graduates. "Nutter got the
idea from Jay Lucker when she worked for him at the Massachusetts Institute
of Technology (MIT) in the late 1980s. 'We won't have a profession if we don't
hire people right out of graduate school,' she quotes Lucker."[4] Think about
partnering with a local library school to offer internships; get involved in helping potential and newer librarians earn the experience they need to succeed.
Also, realize that succession planning can be a factor as early as when making hiring decisions; think about people's long-term potential.

Offer all of your staff members support for continuing education, leadership opportunities, and advancement potential. Succession planning and
retention are not merely generational issues; creating an environment where
all staff can succeed benefits everyone, and creating opportunities for
increased communication and collaboration benefits your institution by
inspiring people's best work. Under-40 survey respondents who worked for
supportive managers and administrations were clear about how this type of
atmosphere benefited them and made them feel as if they were full participants in their institutions and profession. One notes: "At first I felt like an
over-qualified, under-experienced, under-aged intruder who couldn't ever
possibly fit in, but thanks to my current boss, I think that my age has helped
my relationship with the profession. I have been given the respect and confidence I feel I deserve, and in turn, my confidence in myself as a librarian
has grown. I am considered to be a valued employee who has recent qualifications, new ideas, and a diverse way of thinking—all these 'age'-related
skills have worked to my advantage, and my boss has stated that these are
some of the many reasons why she employed me."

Libraries that look at professional development as the first place to cut
funds, or that fail to offer conference attendance or other funding to new professionals or long-term staff—not to mention those that offer them to no one—
lose out in the end. If funds are limited, look for creative ways to stretch
them. Trade off conference attendance, look for local opportunities, and
have people who attend conferences and workshops bring home ideas and
reports to the rest of the staff.

Be flexible and open to new ideas and the possibility of change. Never,
ever use the phrase "we have always done it this way." Pay attention to

varying communication styles, and remember that the same open access to information that we tout for our patrons is also essential to a smoothly functioning staff. Give younger and newer librarians the opportunity to manage projects and take on other leadership positions; this will help them develop skills and help give long-term staff a picture of younger people acting effectively "in charge." Show that you value their input and skills; take the time to find the use for and value in diverse skills and perspectives. Take a page from Beth Wheeler Dean, Head of Youth Services, Huntsville Madison County Public Library, Huntsville, AL, who says of her younger colleagues: "They bring new ideas, new enthusiasm, more energy, and a new network of peers. There is nothing like a pair of new eyes. We just have to remember to keep our mouths shut and let them go. I love seeing the fire in their eyes."

As Marylaine Block writes: "In the face of rapid demographic, technological, and political change, we must do everything we can to make our entire organization smarter and nimbler, which includes hiring and listening to new, young librarians. ... The solution, it seems to me, is to give our new, young librarians what Newhouse and Spisak found they want: 'Huge doses of openness and affirmation ... proper training, adherence to the tenets of librarianship, appropriate feedback and rewards.' Of course they should be respectful and willing to learn from older librarians. But older librarians have the obligation to listen back, and give the newest members of our profession opportunities to put their ideas and enthusiasm into practice."[5] Libraries should naturally evolve along with their newest recruits—in order to remain relevant, the profession needs to incorporate new viewpoints and ideas.

Recognize that generational issues can be a factor in recruitment and retention. Do some reading about generational differences, talk to your younger employees and solicit their input, ask them about their priorities and outlook. Part of your job as a manager is to blend together the talents and outlooks of people from multiple backgrounds. Age is just one factor, but multiple generations can add to the diversity and vibrancy of your library. If your policy has been to "grow your own" by encouraging long-time paraprofessionals to get degrees—which is a great way to build the profession and retain the experience and skills of long-term staff—think of supplementing this approach by also actively soliciting young librarians who are new to the profession.

Library Journal's John N. Berry III writes: "While the body of people recruited [to MLS programs] from libraries is generally diverse and guarantees new librarians with great faith in the profession, it tends to make for an older constituency of students, deeply rooted in libraries as they exist. The library of the future may have difficulty being born in that culture. If the field needs new blood, needs younger librarians who have more of their careers ahead of them and thinking that is brand new and out of the box, it needs a younger generation of recruits to go with the strong librarians brought in from libraries today to create the library of the future."[6] Look at the advantages a fresh perspective can bring. Wilder sees a similar need, saying:

> We may be fortunate that at the very moment that information undergoes its biggest revolution since Gutenberg, librarianship appears positioned to take on substantial numbers of new people with new skills to help it adapt. There may even be a competitive advantage in being obliged to recruit large numbers of young people sooner than comparable professions.
>
> But will these young people change the traditional culture and values of librarianship? Perhaps they will change it for the better. It is helpful to remember the last great generational shift, the staffing boom that brought thousands of people into librarianship in the 1960s. That generation also brought new skills to a changing profession, in ways that now appear to have been healthy, even necessary.
>
> By this view, there is no cause for alarm if today's new hires do not look more like traditional librarians. In fact, the long-term interest of librarianship may make those differences necessary, just as they were for the generation before them. Now, as before, the kids are alright.[7]

Administrators and others interested in retention, recruitment, and the future of our profession might over the next couple of years wish to watch "The Future of Librarians In the Workforce," a two-year IMLS-funded study that will look at anticipated labor shortages and identify approaches to recruiting and retaining the librarians needed to fill these (see www.library workforce.org).

Some NextGens do worry about a backlash from their administrators or colleagues due to too much discussion of generational issues. One says, "It makes me wonder if perhaps the generational difference in librarianship has become a problem because it is discussed so often, rather than the other way around. I can definitely see how it impacts my relationships with the older librarians I work with, and it seems to be largely because they expect me to think that everything new (and young) is better—so then they turn that around and act like anything new is bad, and only people who have worked in libraries for 20 years know anything about anything. It has definitely gotten worse at my current workplace over the past couple of years and it seems like it is because my co-workers/employers have been hearing so much about the potential problem." Try to avoid overreacting to NextGens' concerns or to any discussion of generational issues; the way to resolve any of these issues is by working together and listening to one another.

Younger librarians, of course, have a responsibility to listen to, learn from, and respect their older colleagues and managers, as well as to learn their organizations' culture. However, administrators and managers also have the responsibility to their younger colleagues to listen to and learn from them, as well as to give them the opportunity to grow. This mutual interaction can benefit both sides. One over-40 survey respondent says: "Some (not all) of them are impatient with my generation, and that's good. They seem to be more mobile and unwilling to stay in less than fulfilling work situations (I don't know if this is true from a quantitative viewpoint, but it sure seems that way). That forces my generation to reassess what makes a 'good' librarian, what sort of person we want to retain in our organization, and what we're willing to do to prove that they are valuable to us. Over and over, I see that retention of the best and brightest is not so much a matter of salary and perks, but of providing opportunities and genuine scope for engagement in their work. And I believe that this enthusiasm is upwardly contagious."

As a library manager, part of your responsibility toward your staff is to bring out their best and to respect their individual needs. Paying attention to generational concerns is just one facet of being a good manager; paying attention to generational trends that affect your institution is just one part of securing your library's future.

Endnotes

1. Pixey Anne Mosley, "Shedding the Stereotypes: Librarians in the 21st Century," *The Reference Librarian* 78 (2002): 172.
2. Stanley J. Wilder, *Demographic Change in Academic Librarianship,* Washington, DC: ARL, 2003: xiv. Wilder also notes at several points in his study that other "aging professions," such as nursing and teaching, skew younger than librarianship, although older than the workforce as a whole.
3. Association of College and Research Libraries, Ad Hoc Task Force on Recruitment & Retention Issues, *Recruitment, Retention, and Restructuring: Human Resources in Academic Libraries,* Chicago: ALA, 2002: 17.

4. John N. Berry III, "Librarian of the Year 2005—North Carolina State University Libraries' Susan Nutter," *Library Journal* January 15, 2005. <www.libraryjournal.com/article/CA491141> 1 Feb. 2005.

5. Marylaine Block, "The Right Hand Knoweth Not..." *Ex Libris* 228 (October 1–8, 2004) <http://marylaine.com/exlibris/xlib228.html> 2 April 2005. See also the sidebar interview with Ria Newhouse in Chapter 9.

6. John N. Berry III, "LIS Recruiting: Does It Make the Grade?" *Library Journal* May 1, 2003 <www.libraryjournal.com/article/CA292594> 17 March 2005.

7. Wilder: 57.

Appendix A: Surveys

Quotes and comments throughout this book are taken from two surveys: one for librarians, library workers, and MLS students under age 40, and one for those over 40. The surveys were broken up this way to roughly correspond to the division between Generation X and Y librarians and their Boomer and Veteran colleagues; this division obviously has a degree of arbitrariness, and there are people who balance uncomfortably on the cusp. The surveys were posted online during January/February 2005 and advertised on several e-mail lists and blogs, on the Lisjobs.com Web site, and in the *Info Career Trends* electronic newsletter. Each was prefaced by the following text:

> *Thanks for taking the time to complete this short survey on your experiences with and thoughts on next generation librarianship. By answering these questions, you are giving your permission to be quoted in a forthcoming book from Information Today, as well as in supporting material on the topic (e.g., articles, promotional materials, presentations). Please be sure to indicate if you would like to remain anonymous; identifying details about your institution will then be deleted from quoted answers as well. If you do not wish to answer a particular question, please leave it blank.*

Under-40 Survey

There were 206 respondents to the under-40 survey. Of the 201 who gave a gender, 170 (85 percent) were female and 31 (15 percent) were male.

183

Survey Questions

Your name:

Your e-mail address:

Your sex:

Your age:

If your answers are quoted, would you prefer to remain anonymous? Y/N

Position Title:

Institution:

City:

State (or equiv.):

Do you have an MLS? Y/N

If yes, when/where did you receive your degree?

Year you began working in libraries:

- Do you consider yourself a "next generation librarian?" Why or why not?
- What do you think is unique about younger librarians' situation now, as opposed to when Baby Boomers, for example, first entered the library workplace?
- How do you think your age affects your relationship with the profession?
- What do you share with older colleagues who have just entered the profession? How does your experience differ?
- What, if anything, was surprising to you about your first library position?
- What do you see as the most pressing issues affecting our profession today?
- Why did you choose to enter the field?
- What steps do you take to remain connected to other librarians? To the profession?
- How does the stereotypical librarian image affect your relationship with the profession? Are there ways in which you personally try to challenge or reclaim this image?
- What impact do you think that NextGen librarians are having/will have on the profession? What unique qualities do they bring to the field?
- Have you considered leaving the profession and taking your skills to another field? Why or why not?
- What would you like to address about generational issues and librarianship that I haven't asked?
- Would you like to be notified via e-mail when the book comes out? Y/N

Over-40 Survey

There were 134 respondents to the over-40 survey. Of the 130 who provided gender, 19 (15 percent) were male and 111 (85 percent) female.

A number of over-40 respondents were upset by the direction of and assumptions behind the survey questions, pointing out that some should have been directed to new grads, regardless of age. Some took advantage of the last "what would you like to address that I haven't asked" question to remedy the situation. They have a point, showing the ease of perceptions creeping in to affect our actions. Were I to redo the survey now, I would include questions specifically targeting older new grads. Others, though, felt the entire concept of "next generation librarians" and of the book itself was ageist in its intent—this concern is addressed in Chapter 1.

Survey Questions

Your name:

Your e-mail address:

Your sex:

Your age:

If your answers are quoted, would you prefer to remain anonymous? Y/N

Position Title:

Institution:

City:

State (or equiv.):

Do you have an MLS? Y/N

If yes, when/where did you receive your degree?

Year you began working in libraries:

- What do you think is unique about younger librarians' situation now, as opposed to when you and/or your colleagues first entered the library workplace?
- How do you think your age affects your relationship with the profession?
- What advice would you give to next generation librarians as they settle in to their careers?
- What advice would you give to next generation librarians who move into management?
- What do you see as the most pressing issues affecting our profession today?
- Why did you choose to enter the field?

- What steps do you take to remain connected to other librarians? To the profession?
- How does the stereotypical librarian image affect your relationship with the profession? Are there ways in which you try to challenge or reclaim this image? Do you see next generation librarians challenging this image?
- What impact do you think that NextGen librarians are having/will have on the profession? What, if any, unique qualities do you think that they bring to the field?
- Have you considered leaving the profession and taking your skills to another field? Why or why not? Are you concerned about younger librarians leaving the field?
- What would you like to address about generational issues and librarianship that I haven't asked?
- Would you like to be notified via e-mail when the book comes out? Y/N

Appendix B: Web Sites

Web sites are listed in the order they appeared in each chapter. URLs are subject to change, and will be updated as available on the book's companion Web site at www.lisjobs.com/nextgen/.

Chapter 1

Recruitment & Retirement: A Deeper Look, www.ala.org/ala/ors/reports/recruitretire/recruitretire-adeeperlook.pdf

Census 2000 EEO Data Tool, www.census.gov/eeo2000/index.html

Chapter 2

ALISE Statistics, http://ils.unc.edu/ALISE/

ALA-Accredited Schools, www.ala.org/ala/education/accredprograms/accreditedprograms.htm

ALA Accreditation Process, www.ala.org/process/

MLA: Schools offering health sciences librarianship coursework, www.mlanet.org/education/libschools/index.html

librarian_wannabes, http://groups.yahoo.com/group/librarian_wannabes/

IU (Indiana University) SLIS, www.livejournal.com/community/iu_slis/

Librarians in Training, www.livejournal.com/community/libraryschool/

Library Grrrls, www.livejournal.com/community/library_grrls/

Library Lovers, www.livejournal.com/community/libraries/

Librarygrads, www.livejournal.com/community/librarygrads/

San Jose State University's SLIS Student Union, www.miraflor.tv/bbs/

Financial Assistance for Library and Information Studies, www.ala.org/ala/hrdr/educprofdev/financialassistance.htm

AALL Scholarships, www.aallnet.org/services/scholarships.asp

ALA Scholarships, www.ala.org/Template.cfm?Section=scholarships

Beta Phi Mu Scholarships, www.beta-phi-mu.org/scholarships.html

MLA Scholarships, www.mlanet.org/awards/grants/index.html

NASIG Awards, www.nasig.org/awards

SLA Scholarships, www.sla.org/content/learn/scholarship/index.cfm

Chapter 3

LIBJOBS, http://infoserv.inist.fr/wwsympa.fcgi/arc/libjobs/

Library Job Postings on the Internet, www.libraryjobpostings.org

Lisjobs.com, www.lisjobs.com

NMRT Resume Review Service, www.geocities.com/nmrtrrs/jobseekers.html

American Association of Law Libraries, Job Hotline, www.aallnet.org/hotline

Michigan Library Association Jobline, www.mla.lib.mi.us/development/jobline.html

Nebraska and Regional Library Jobs, www.nlc.state.ne.us/libjob/adjobs.html

Society of American Archivists, Online Employment Bulletin, www.archivists.org/employment/index.asp

The Chronicle of Higher Education, http://chronicle.com/jobs/300/100/6000/

Library Journal, http://jobs.libraryjournal.com

American Libraries, www.ala.org/ala/education/empopps/careerleadsb/careerleadsonline.htm

Lisjobs.com, Interview Advice, www.lisjobs.com/advice.htm#interview

Writing a CV, http://ucblibraries.colorado.edu/internal/fac/V.D.5_cv.pdf

Lisjobs.com, Temp and Employment Agencies, www.lisjobs.com/temp.htm

Lisjobs.com, Salary Statistics, www.lisjobs.com/advice.htm#stats

Chapter 5

ALA's Continuing Education Clearinghouse, www.ala.org/ce/

BCR, www.bcr.org/training/workshops/web-based.html

Beyond the Job, http://librarycareers.blogspot.com

Dynix Institute, www.dynix.com/institute/

InfoPeople, www.infopeople.org/training/

PALINET, www.palinet.org/services/edprogram/catalog/onlinecalendar.asp?Type=online

SLA Online Learning, www.sla.org/content/learn/learnmore/index.cfm

WebJunction, www.webjunction.org

University of Maryland's College of Information Studies, CE Courses, www.clis.umd.edu/ce/index.html

Chapter 6

The Fashionista Librarian, www.geocities.com/fashionistalibrarian/

ALA's Gay, Lesbian, Bisexual, and Transgendered Roundtable, www.ala.org/ala/glbtrt/welcomeglbtround.htm

GAY-LIBN, www-lib.usc.edu/~trimmer/gay-libn.html

ALA's Office for Diversity, www.ala.org/diversity/

American Indian Library Association, www.nativeculturelinks.com/aila.html

Asian/Pacific American Librarians Association, www.apalaweb.org

Black Caucus of the American Library Association (BCALA), www.bcala.org

Chinese American Librarians Association (CALA), www.cala-web.org

REFORMA (The National Association to Promote Library and Information Services to Latinos and the Spanish-Speaking), www.reforma.org

ALA's Spectrum Scholarships, www.ala.org/spectrum/

ARL (Association of Research Libraries) Initiative to Recruit a Diverse Workforce, www.arl.org/diversity/initapp2005.pdf

Diversity Librarians' Network, Scholarships and Awards List, www.lib.utk.edu/residents/dln/scholarships.html

Knowledge River (University of Arizona), http://knowledgeriver.arizona.edu

ALA Diversity Research Grant Program, www.ala.org/ala/diversity/divresearchgrants/diversityresearch.htm

Cornell University Library Fellows Program, www.library.cornell.edu/diversity

University of Tennessee Minority Librarian Residency Program, www.lib.utk.edu/lss/lpp/minres.html

Chapter 7

Pop Goes the Library, www.popgoesthelibrary.com

AliaNEWGRAD, http://lists.alia.org.au/mailman/listinfo/aliaNEWGRAD/

IFLA's NPDG-L (New Professionals Discussion Group Mailing List), http://infoserv.inist.fr/wwsympa.fcgi/info/npdg-l

Nexgenlib-l, http://lists.topica.com/lists/nexgenlib-l

NEWLIB-L, www.lahacal.org/newlib/

NMRT-L, www.ala.org/ala/nmrt/nmrtmailinglists.htm

The Young Librarian (TYL), www.younglibrarian.net

Unofficial ALA Conference Blog, http://meredith.wolfwater.com/wiki/

SLA's "Tips From an Experienced Conference-Goer," www.sla.org/content/Events/conference/ac2005/geninfo/tips.cfm

AALL (American Association of Law Libraries) Grants Program, www.aallnet.org/committee/grants/grants.asp

ALA Grants and Fellowships, www.ala.org/Template.cfm?Section=grant fellowship

IFLA (International Federation of Library Associations and Institutions) Fellowships, Grants, and Awards, www.ifla.org/III/members/grants.htm

NASIG (North American Serials Interest Group) Student Grant, www.nasig.org/awards/timedated/studentgrant.html

MLA (Medical Library Association), www.mlanet.org/awards/grants/index.html

New York METRO's New Librarians Special Interest Group, http://metro.org/SIGs/newlibs.html

ALIA New Generation Policy and Advisory Group, www.alia.org.au/governance/committees/new.generation/

ALIA New Librarians Symposia, http://conferences.alia.org.au/newlibrarian 2004/

Chapter 8

Librariansahm, http://groups.yahoo.com/group/librariansahm/

Libparenting, http://groups.yahoo.com/group/libparenting/

Chapter 9

The Young Librarian, www.younglibrarian.net

The Young Librarian Weblog, http://younglibrarian.blogspot.com

Endangered Libraries, http://librarydust.typepad.com/library_dust/2005/01/endangered_libr.html

ALA: Library Funding, www.ala.org/ala/news/libraryfunding/libraryfunding.htm

Trading Spaces, www.sjrlc.org/tradingspaces/

FreeCulture, http://freeculture.org

Lawrence Lessig's blog, www.lessig.org/blog/

Chapter 10

The Future of Librarians in the Workforce, www.libraryworkforce.org

Recommended Reading

Abif, Khafre and Teresa Y. Neely. *In Our Own Voices: The Changing Face of Librarianship.* Lanham, MD: Scarecrow, 1996.

Abram, Stephen. "Dealing With the Generations: New (and Free) Must-Read Studies." *Information Outlook* 7:1 (January 2003): 46.

Abram, Stephen. "The Value of Libraries: Impact, Normative Data, & Influencing Funders." *SIRSI OneSource* 1:5 (May 2005). <www.imakenews.com/sirsi/e_article000396335.cfm> 25 May 2005.

Abram, Stephen and Judy Luther. "Born With the Chip." *Library Journal* May 1 2004: 34-7.

Arant, Wendi and Candace R. Benefiel. *The Image and Role of the Librarian.* Binghamton, NY: Haworth, 2002.

Association of College and Research Libraries, Ad Hoc Task Force on Recruitment & Retention Issues. *Recruitment, Retention, and Restructuring: Human Resources in Academic Libraries.* Chicago: ALA, 2002.

Bellman, Geoffrey. *Getting Things Done When You Are Not In Charge: How To Succeed From a Support Position.* San Francisco: Berrett-Koehler, 1992.

Bennis, Warren G. and Robert J. Thomas. *Geeks & Geezers: How Era, Values, and Defining Moments Shape Leaders.* Boston: Harvard Business School Press, 2002.

Bernstein, Albert and Sydney Craft Rozen. *Dinosaur Brains: Dealing With All Those Impossible People at Work.* New York: Wiley, 1989.

Berry, John N. III. "LIS Recruiting: Does It Make the Grade?" *Library Journal* May 1 2003. <www.libraryjournal.com/article/CA292594> 17 March 2005.

Berry, John N. III. "Memo To Baby Boomers." *Library Journal* June 1 2004: 12.

Block, Marylaine. "The Right Hand Knoweth Not..." *Ex Libris* 228 (October 1-8, 2004). <http://marylaine.com/exlibris/exlib228.html> 2 April 2005.

Bobrovitz, Jennifer and Rosemary Griebel. "Still Mousy After All These Years: The Image of the Librarian in the 21st Century." *Feliciter* 47:5 (2001): 260-3.

Bonnette, Ashley E. "Mentoring Minority Librarians Up the Career Ladder." *Library Administration & Management* 18:3 (Summer 2004): 134-9.

Bridges, Karl, ed. *Expectations of Librarians in the 21st Century.* Westport, CT: Greenwood, 2003.

Central Jersey Regional Library Cooperative. Become a Librarian! 2001-2005. <www.becomealibrarian.org> 22 May 2005.

Cooper, Julie F. and Eric A. Cooper. "Generational Dynamics and Librarianship: Managing Generation X." *Illinois Libraries* 80:1 (Winter 1998): 18-21.

Crosby, Olivia. "Librarians: Information Experts in the Information Age." *Occupational Outlook Quarterly* Winter 2000-01. <www.bls.gov/opub/ooq/2000/Winter/art01.pdf> March 13 2005.

Cross, Robb and Andrew Parker. *The Hidden Power of Social Networks: Understanding How Work Really Gets Done in Organizations.* Boston: HBS Press, 2004.

Cunningham, Nancy. "In Search of an Emotionally Healthy Library." LISCareer.com. December 2001 <liscareer.com/cunningham_ eiq.htm> 9 December 2004.

DeCandido, GraceAnne. "Ten Graces for New Librarians." Commencement address, School of Information Science and Policy, SUNY/Albany, Sunday, May 19, 1996. <www.well.com/user/ ladyhawk/albany.html> 11 February 2005.

Edmonson, Emily (pseud.). "Checking Out Her Options." *The Chronicle of Higher Education* September 30 2004 <chronicle.com/jobs/ 2004/09/2004093001c.htm> 9 December 2004.

Edmonson, Emily (pseud.). "Raising My Standards." *The Chronicle of Higher Education* February 2 2005 <http://chronicle.com/jobs/ 2005/02/2005020201c.htm> 5 February 2005.

Families and Work Institute. "Generation & Gender In the Workplace." American Business Collaboration, October 2004. <http://familiesandwork.org/eproducts/genandgender.pdf> 17 March 2005.

Foot, David K., with Daniel Stoffman. *Boom, Bust & Echo: How to Profit From the Coming Demographic Shift.* Toronto: Macfarlane, 1996.

GenTrends. Monthly newsletter. <www.gentrends.com/newsletter.html> 10 March 2005.

Gillon, Steve. *Boomer Nation.* New York: Free Press, 2004.

Gordon, Rachel Singer. *The Accidental Library Manager.* Medford, NJ: Information Today, Inc., 2005.

Grady, Jenifer and Tracie Hall. "The World Is Changing: Why Aren't We? Recruiting Minorities to Librarianship." *Library Worklife* 1:4 (April 2004) <www.ala-apa.org/newsletter/vol1no4/recruitment.html> 22 May 2005.

Greene, Kelly. "Many Older Professionals Delay Their Retirement." *CareerJournal.com* October 2 2003. <www.careerjournal.com/myc/retirement/20031002-greene.html> 22 May 2005.

Hernon, Peter, Ronald R. Powell, and Arthur P. Young. *The Next Library Leadership: Attributes of Academic and Public Library Directors.* Westport, CT: Libraries Unlimited, 2003.

Houghton, Sarah. "Are You Sure You're a Librarian?" <http://librarianinblack.typepad.com/librarianinblack/files/Areyousure.pdf> 22 May 2005.

Howe, Neil and William Strauss. *Millennials Rising: The Next Great Generation.* New York: Vintage, 2000.

Hutley, Sue and Terena Solomons. "Generational Change in Australian Librarianship: Viewpoints From Generation X." Paper presented at ALIA 2004, 21–24 Sept. 2004 <http://conferences.alia.org.au/alia2004/pdfs/hutley.s.paper.pdf> 29 January 2005.

Jacobsen, Teresa L. "The Class of 1988." *Library Journal* July 2004: 38–41.

Jacobson, Jennifer. "A Shortage of Academic Librarians." *The Chronicle of Higher Education* August 14, 2002 <http://chronicle.com/jobs/2002/08/2002081401c.htm> 2 Feb. 2005.

KALIPER Advisory Committee, Association for Library and Information Science Education (ALISE). "Educating Library and Information Science Professionals for a New Century: The KALIPER Report, Executive Summary." Reston, VA: ALISE, 2000. <www.alise.org/publications/kaliper.pdf> 16 March 2005.

Kneale, Ruth A. "You Don't Look Like a Librarian!" <www.librarian-image.net> 22 May, 2005.

Lancaster, Lynne C. "The Click and Clash of Generations." *Library Journal* Oct. 15 2003. <www.libraryjournal.com/article/CA325060> 22 May, 2005.

Lancaster, Lynne C. and David Stillman. *When Generations Collide: Who They Are. Why They Clash. How To Solve the Generational Puzzle at Work.* New York: HarperBusiness, 2002.

Larsen, Suzanne T. and Joan S. McConkey. "Applying for Professional Positions." *C&RL News* June 1995: 415–417.

Lenzini, Rebecca T. and Carolyn Lipscomb. "The Graying of the Library Profession: A Survey of Our Professional Associations and Their Responses." *Searcher* July/August 2002: 88–97.

Lubans, John Jr. "Leading From the Middle." *Library Administration & Management* 18:4 (Fall 2004): 205–7.

Lynch, Mary Jo. "Reaching 65: Lots of Librarians Will Be There Soon." *American Libraries* March 2002: 55–6.

Lynch, Mary Jo. "Recruitment and Retirement: A Deeper Look." *American Libraries* January 2005: 28.

Lynch, Mary Jo. "What We Now Know About Librarians." *American Libraries* February 2000: 8–9.

Lynch, Mary Jo, Stephen Tordella, and Thomas Godfrey. "Recruitment and Retirement: A Deeper Look." Chicago: ALA, 2005. <www.ala.org/ala/ors/reports/recruitretire/recruitretire-adeeperlook.pdf > 20 April 2005.

Macko, Lia and Kerry Rubin. *Midlife Crisis at 30.* New York: Rodale, 2004.

Matarazzo, James M. "Library Human Resources: The Y2K Plus 10 Challenge." *The Journal of Academic Librarianship* 26:4 (2000): 223–4.

Matarazzo, James M. "Who Wants To Be a Millionaire (Sic Librarian!)." *The Journal of Academic Librarianship* 26:5 (2000): 309–10.

Matarazzo, James M. and Joseph J. Mika. "Workforce Planning for Library and Information Science." *Library & Information Science Research* 26:2 (2004): 115–20.

May, Susan Basalla with Risa Nystrom McDonell. "Coffee in 2002, a Job Offer in 2004." *The Chronicle of Higher Education* Jan. 20 2005 <http://chronicle.com/jobs/2005/01/2005012001c.htm> 12 February 2005.

Millett, Michelle S. and Lisa Pozas. "Recruitment and Retention of New Academic Librarians in Their Own Words: Who They Are and What They Want." 2005. <www.trinity.edu/mmillet/professional/NewLibProject.htm> 21 May 2005

Moran, Robert F. "A View From the Ranks: An Interview With Dorothy A. Moran, Paraprofessional, Liverpool (N.Y.) Public Library." *Library Administration & Management* 18:4 (Fall 2004): 176–8.

Mosley, Pixey Anne. "Shedding the Stereotype: Librarians in the 21st Century." *The Reference Librarian* 78 (2002): 167–76.

Mosley, Pixey Anne. *Transitioning From Librarian to Middle Manager.* Westport, CT: Libraries Unlimited, 2004.

Nesbeitt, Sarah and Rachel Singer Gordon. *The Information Professional's Guide to Career Development Online.* Medford, NJ: Information Today, Inc., 2002.

Newhouse, Ria and April Spisak. "Fixing the First Job." *Library Journal* August 15 2004 <www.libraryjournal.com/article/CA443916> 9 December 2004.

"NextGen." Monthly column, *Library Journal* <www.libraryjournal.com/community/891/NextGen/42861.html> 22 May 2005.

Oblinger, Diana. "Boomers, Gen-Xers, and Millennials: Understanding the New Students." *Educause* July/August 2003: 37–45 <www.educause.edu/ir/library/pdf/erm0342.pdf>. 22 May 2005.

Oblinger, Diana G. and James L. Oblinger, eds. *Educating the Net Generation.* Educause, February 2005. <www.educause.edu/educatingthenetgen/> 22 May 2005.

Pankl, Robert R. "Baby Boom Generation Librarians." *Library Management* 24: 4/5 (2004): 215–222.

Patterson, Linda. "The Face of the Library." *Library Journal* Feb. 15 2004: 42–3.

Raines, Claire. *Beyond Generation X: A Practical Guide for Managers.* Menlo Park, CA: Crisp, 1997.

Raines, Claire. *Connecting Generations: The Sourcebook for a New Workplace.* Menlo Park, CA: Crisp, 2003.

Robbins, Alexandra. *Conquering Your Quarterlife Crisis: Advice From Twentysomethings Who Have Been There and Survived.* New York: Penguin, 2004.

Robbins, Alexandra and Abby Wilner. *Quarterlife Crisis: The Unique Challenges of Life in Your Twenties.* New York: Penguin, 2001.

Roberts, Amanda. "Combating Ageism: Lessons Learned by 'Baby' Librarians." *NMRT Footnotes* Nov. 2003. Reprint available at LISCareer.com. <www.liscareer.com/roberts_ageism.htm> 22 May 2005.

Rodgers, Lala. "Early Career Survival." *Library Journal* May 1 2004: 40–1.

Rogers, Michael. "Tackling Recruitment." *Library Journal* Feb. 1 2003 <www.libraryjournal.com/article/CA270644.html> 17 March 2005.

Rogers, Michael. "Talking To the Wall." *Library Journal* June 1 2004: 94, 96.

Rogers, Michael. "Where Are All the Library Jobs?" *Library Journal* September 15 2004: 14–15.

Ross, Catherine Sheldrick and Patricia Dewdney. *Communicating Professionally: A How-To-Do-It Manual for Library Applications, 2nd ed.* New York: Neal-Schuman, 1998.

Saunders, Laura. "Navigating a Tight Job Market: There's a Job For You." *C&RL News* 64:10 (November 2003): 661–663, 669.

Scales, B. Jane. "A Neo-Modern Summary of the Futcha: An Exploration of the Generation X in Our Midst." *The Reference Librarian* 64 (1999): 21–30.

Shontz, Priscilla K. *Jump Start Your Career in Library and Information Science.* Lanham, MD: Scarecrow, 2002.

Shontz, Priscilla K., ed. *The Librarian's Career Guidebook.* Lanham, MD: Scarecrow, 2004.

Silver, Samantha. "Can't We All Just Get Along? Bridging Generation Gaps in Libraries." LISCareer.com, March 2005 <www.liscareer.com/silver_generation.htm> 3 April 2005.

Singer, Paula, Jeanne Goodrich, and Linda Goldberg. "Your Library's Future." *Library Journal* October 15 2004: 38–40.

Sloan, Bernie. "Changes in LIS Education: A Bibliography." Rev. October 2, 2004. <www.lis.uiuc.edu/~b-sloan/edbib.html> 22 May 2005.

Smith, J. Walker and Ann Clurman. *Rocking the Ages: The Yankelovich Report on Generational Marketing.* New York: HarperBusiness, 1997.

Squire, Kurt and Constance Steinkuhler. "Meet the Gamers." *Library Journal* April 15 2005. <www.libraryjournal.com/article/CA516033> 22 May 2005.

St. Lifer, Evan. "The Boomer Brain Drain: The Last of a Generation?" *Library Journal* May 1 2000: 38–42.

Steffen, Nicolle, et al. *Retirement, Retention, and Recruitment: The Future of Librarianship in Colorado.* Denver, CO: Library Research Service, September 2004. <www.lrs.org/documents/closer_look/RRR_web.pdf> 12 February 2005.

Storey, Tom and Carrie Lauer. "The Next Generation of Librarians." *OCLC Newsletter* April-May-June 2004: 8-13 <www.oclc.org/news/publications/newsletters/oclc/2004/264/default.html> 11 May 2005.

Stout, Nancy. "Profession on the Verge of a Nervous Breakdown." *The Serials Librarian* 47:1–2 (2004): 45–55.

Strauss, William and Neil Howe. *13th Gen: Abort, Retry, Ignore, Fail?* New York: Vintage, 1993.

Tapscott, Don. *Growing Up Digital: The Rise of the Net Generation.* New York: McGraw-Hill, 1998.

Tennant, Roy. "Strategies for Keeping Current." *Library Journal* Sept. 15 2003: 28.

Tenopir, Carol. "Educating Tomorrow's Information Professionals Today." *Searcher* July/August 2002. <www.infotoday.com/searcher/jul02/tenopir.htm> 17 March 2005.

Tulgan, Bruce. *Managing Generation X: How To Bring Out the Best in Young Talent, rev. & updated ed.* New York: Norton, 2000, 1996.

Tulgan, Bruce and Carolyn A. Martin. *Managing Generation Y: Global Citizens Born in the Late Seventies and Early Eighties.* Amherst: HRD Press, 2001.

Tulgan, Bruce and Carolyn A. Martin. *Managing the Generation Mix: From Collision to Collaboration.* Amherst: HRD Press, 2002.

Urgo, Marisa. *Developing Information Leaders: Harnessing the Talents of Generation X.* London: Bowker Saur, 2000.

Urgo, Marisa. "No Slackers Here!" *Information Outlook* 2:4 (April 1998): 29–32.

Watkins, Christine. "Can Librarians Play Basketball?" *American Libraries* March 1999: 58–61.

Watkins, Christine. "A Community Mirror: Reflections on the Color of Librarianship." *American Libraries* November 1999: 64–6.

Watkins, Michael. *The First 90 Days: Critical Success Strategies for New Leaders at All Levels.* Boston: Harvard Business School, 2003.

Whelan, Debra Lau. "The Only Young School Librarian?" *School Library Journal* May 2003: 52–5.

Wilcox, Matt. "Why I Won't Hire You." LISCareer.com, December 2004 <www.liscareer.com/wilcox_wonthire.htm>. 26 January 2005.

Wilder, Stanley J. *The Age Demographics of Professional Librarians: A Profession Apart.* Washington DC: Association of Research Libraries, 1995.

Wilder, Stanley J. *Demographic Change in Academic Librarianship.* Association of Research Libraries, Washington, DC: 2003.

Wilder, Stanley J. "Generational Change and the Niche for Librarians." *The Journal of Academic Librarianship* 22:5 (Sept. 1996): 385–6.

Young, Arthur and Steve Casburn. "Gen X Bites Back." *American Libraries* Sept. 2004: 43–5.

Young, Arthur, Peter Hernon, and Ronald Powell. "What Will Gen Next Need to Lead?" *American Libraries* May 2004: 33–5.

Zemke, Ron. "Generations at Work." *Executive Update* Feb. 2001. <www.centeronline.org/knowledge/article.cfm?ID=615&> 5 March 2005.

Zemke, Ron, Claire Raines, and Bob Filipczak. *Generations at Work: Managing the Clash of Veterans, Boomers, Xers, and Nexters in Your Workplace.* New York: AMACOM, 2000.

About the Author

Rachel Singer Gordon is the former Head of Computer Services at the Franklin Park Public Library in Illinois, and is currently Consulting Editor for the Book Publishing Division of Information Today, Inc. She is the founder and Webmaster of the library career site Lisjobs.com, from which she also publishes *Info Career Trends,* a free, bimonthly electronic newsletter on career development issues for librarians. With Sarah Johnson, Rachel maintains "Beyond the Job," a professional development Weblog for information professionals. Rachel also writes the monthly "Computer Media" column for *Library Journal*, and is a frequent contributor to *LJ's* "NextGen" column. She writes the monthly "Publish, Don't Perish" column for Emerald's Library Link, and coauthors the "Tech Tips for Every Librarian" department for *Computers in Libraries* magazine.

Rachel has written and presented widely on career development issues for librarians. Her published work includes *The Information Professional's Guide to Career Development Online* (with Sarah Nesbeitt, ITI, 2002), *The Accidental Systems Librarian* (ITI, 2003), *The Librarian's Guide to Writing for Publication* (Scarecrow, 2004), and *The Accidental Library Manager* (ITI, 2005). She holds an MLIS from Dominican University and an MA from Northwestern University.

Index

More Great Books from Information Today, Inc.

The Information Professional's Guide to Career Development Online

By Sarah L. Nesbeitt and Rachel Singer Gordon

This book is designed to meet the needs of librarians interested in using online tools to advance their careers. It offers practical advice on topics ranging from current awareness services and personal Web pages to distance education, electronic resumes, and online job searches. New librarians will learn how to use the Internet to research education opportunities, and experienced info pros will learn new ways to network.

416 pp/softbound/ISBN 1-57387-124-9 $29.50

The Successful Academic Librarian
Winning Strategies from Library Leaders

Edited by Gwen Meyer Gregory

While every academic librarian works to meet the research needs of faculty and students, many are expected to assume other obligations as part of a faculty or tenure system. If this were not enough to test a librarian's mettle, the widely varying academic focuses and cultures of college and university libraries almost certainly will. This book, expertly edited by academic librarian, writer, and speaker Gwen Meyer Gregory, is an antidote to the stress and burnout that almost every academic librarian experiences at one time or another. Gregory and nearly 20 of her peers and mentors take a practical approach to a full range of critical topics facing the profession.

256 pp/hardbound/ISBN 1-57387-232-6 $39.50

The Accidental Library Manager

By Rachel Singer Gordon

In *The Accidental Library Manager*, Rachel Singer Gordon provides support for new managers, aspiring managers, and those who find themselves in unexpected management roles. Gordon fills in the gaps left by brief and overly theoretical library school coursework, showing library managers how to be more effective in their positions and how to think about their work in terms of the goals of their larger institutions. Included are insights from working library managers at different levels and in various types of libraries addressing a wide range of management issues and situations.

384 pp/softbound/ISBN 1-57387-210-5 $29.50

Net Effects
How Librarians Can Manage the Unintended Consequences of the Internet

Edited by Marylaine Block

The Internet is a mixed blessing for libraries and librarians. On the one hand, it provides opportunities to add services and expand collections; on the other, it has increased user expectations and contributed to techno stress. In *Net Effects*, librarian, journalist, and Internet guru Marylaine Block examines the issues and brings together a wealth of insights, war stories, and solutions. Nearly 50 articles by dozens of imaginative librarians—expertly selected, annotated, and integrated by the editor—suggest practical and creative ways to deal with the range of Internet "side effects," regain control of the library, and avoid being blindsided by technology again.

380 pp/hardbound/ISBN 1-57387-171-0 $39.50